THE BUSINESS

WRITING GUIDE

Becoming an Expert with Words – Plus Templates & Samples Emails for Work, Cold Calling, and Building a Business.

DR. ABI DEMI

Table of Contents

DEDICATION

I dedicate this body of work to my darling wife Zee, to my parents Arc. Mikhail and Sade. Without these pillars, I am naught. Finally, to all my friends, teachers, mentors. Thank you; it truly takes a village.

ABOUT THIS BOOK

This work is a distilled brain box of 10 years of business writing experience garnered from several platforms, multiple industries and real life scenarios of what works and what doesn't.

This book covers the fundamentals of good business writing, from the basics of grammar and punctuation to the essentials of style and organization. It explains how to write for different audiences, how to structure a document to convey maximum information, and how to use language to persuade and influence.

With its clear instructions and practical advice, it gives you the confidence and skills to write better and with more impact. Whether you're a student, business owner, a professional writer, or just looking to get your first job/promotion, this book will help you become a more effective communicator.

ABOUT THIS AUTHOR

Dr Abi Demi is an experienced digital marketing consultant, technical copywriter and business development executive with expertise in Information Technology, content marketing, amd enterprise development.

He typifies the typical on-net entrepreneur story- rising from the trenches of freelance platforms to founding a copywriting and marketing tech agency that has served over 1000 clients and executed over 5000 projects. He shares some of his works, opinions and think pieces on his mindset and business hub known as Fortified Thinking dot com.

He is an author of several books and has collaborated in several capacities (content, technology, marketing, consultation) for brands like Block Leaders, ItemBanc, CCN, Crestonium, S3ntigraph, Didofa, Pharmaclinix, BaublesnBloom, ReAble and more.

After bagging his doctorate in Commerce, He delved into consultation and public speaking. Dr. Abi Demi has spoken and attended seminars, workshops and conferences locally and internationally. When Demi is not creating business reports, or

building landing pages, you can find him supporting his favorite club; Arsenal FC, or watching (and rewatching) his favorite TV series – Game of Thrones."

MY CREDO

WHO AM I

I am a bag of flesh and soul.

I am a figment of young and old.

I am a body of love and lust.

I am neither found nor lost.

WHO AM I?

I am a mix of cold and warmth.

I am a reflection of light and darkness.

I am a slight of linger and touch.

I am an apprentice and a master.

WHO AM I?

I am a mold of perfection and Flaws.

I am a shade of black and white.

I am a shroud of mystery and simplicity.

I am a produce of day and night.

WHO AM I?

I am evolution and extinction.

I am he who shall emerge and extinguish.

I am a pillar of the life that glitters distinction.

I am a man in many for all to relinquish.

MY MESSAGE TO YOU

Writing is an art form in itself.

I started my journey as a writer doodling phrases and writing short poems. Enamored by my skills, I buried myself into the literary works of Charles Dickens, Chinua Achebe, Wole Soyinka, Shakespeare, and several other great writers.

Learning the artsy part of writing helped shape my story telling ability so when it was time to transition into business writing, I didn't struggle as much.

When I started my MBA degree, I began a freelance copywriting and marketing agency that offered several forms of business content related services like white paper production, landing page, email copy, website content, CV/Resume writing. I honed my business writing by studying the greats like David Ogilvy, Russel Bronson and Eugene Schwartz.

As an independent contractor and through my agency, I worked with and for clients across several industries including finance, technology, healthcare, real estate, e-commerce, and more.

During this period till date:

- Invested $15,000+ of real money into polishing his craft
- Passed 10,000+ hours of practice time.
- Earns six figures as proof of value delivery

Writing allows me to share my view of the world and to have a platform to express my opinions. It helps me to develop my communication skills and to better understand the world around me. It can also be an important outlet for stress relief, which is important in this fast-paced world. Ultimately, writing is my passion because it allows me to express myself in a way that is both meaningful and powerful.

You don't have to love writing; you just need to know how to make it work for you. Writing is the highest form of soft power. In the earlier centuries, military might and nuclear capacity dictated who rules the world.

Soft power rules the world today. The pen has never been mightier than the sword than right now.

PAGE LEFT BLANK FOR JOURNALS AND JOTTING

CHAPTER 1-
WORDS ARE
POWERFUL

Understanding Business Writing

During my final year of my bachelor's degree, I was eager to dive into the world of writing. I had always enjoyed expressing my thoughts on paper, but little did I know that my passion for writing would lead me to discover the distinct field of business writing and article writing.

It all began during a particularly enlightening class on professional communication. Our professor introduced us to the concept of business writing, emphasizing its significance in the corporate world.

He explained that business writing was more than just conveying information; it was about crafting persuasive and succinct messages that could influence decision-making. The clarity and precision required in this form of writing intrigued me, and I saw its immense value in the professional world.

Fast forward to 3 years later, I embarked on my MBA journey. As I delved deeper into my studies, I met like-minded individuals who shared my passion for writing. Among them were Jire Jacob and Abiola, two friends who would become integral to my growth in the trade.

Jire Jacob, a seasoned business professional, had a knack for crafting compelling business proposals and reports. He took me under his wing and showed me the ropes of business writing. He shared valuable tips on how to structure emails, create persuasive marketing materials, and draft comprehensive business reports. Learning from him, I realized that business writing demanded a unique skill set—one that could captivate readers and drive them to take action.

On the other hand, Abiola was a digital marketer passionate about storytelling and capturing the essence of human experiences. His expertise was in article writing, where he skillfully weaved narratives

that touched hearts and shed light on pressing issues. I admired his ability to evoke emotions through his words and his dedication to uncovering truth and sharing knowledge.

As I straddled between my MBA classes and bonding with my friends, I noticed the contrasting aspects of business writing and article writing. Business writing required a more structured and formal approach, focusing on achieving specific objectives, while article writing allowed for creativity and freedom of expression.

The differences between the two styles became more apparent as I honed my skills in both worlds. I realized that my background in business writing complemented my MBA studies, enabling me to communicate effectively in a professional setting. Meanwhile, my exposure to article writing fueled my passion for storytelling, inspiring me to pursue writing opportunities outside the corporate world.

Throughout my journey, Jire Jacob and Abiola became more than just friends; they became mentors and kindred spirits. They challenged me to push the boundaries of my writing and offered valuable insights that shaped my understanding of the craft.

The world of business is changing at a rapid pace, and it's important for everyone in the workplace to be able to communicate effectively.

Business writing is the practice of writing letters, reports, e-mails and other materials in a professional setting. It includes all forms of communication that you do with other people in your business or organization. Business documents also include letters, memos and e-mails.

Business writing is an important asset in any workplace because it enables you to communicate clearly and effectively. By improving your skills at business communications you can improve relationships with customers or clients by increasing trustworthiness as well as gaining new customers who value what you have to say about their product or service offering

Business writing helps you communicate your message clearly and effectively by providing the right information to the right person at the right time.

Being able to communicate information in a concise and clear manner helps streamline processes and reduces confusion for all stakeholders.

When you think of business writing, what comes to mind?

Maybe you picture a memo or email with lots of unnecessary verbiage. In reality, though, business writing should be clear and concise. This means that your messages are easy to understand and can be easily processed by those who receive them.

Concise writing saves time because it cuts out unnecessary words that could be spent elsewhere in the message (such as repeating something). The fewer words there are, the less work someone has to do when reading through your document; this makes them more likely to read everything on one page instead of flipping back and forth multiple times trying to figure out what was said originally.

Concise writing also reduces confusion for all stakeholders involved because it's easier for everyone involved in a process—from executives down through employees—to see exactly what needs done next or where things stand at any given moment due to how much information has already been given out from previous conversations between parties before getting into this new one now happening between them!

Successful business writing also demonstrates your ability to craft a logical argument that can be easily followed by your reader. This is crucial for any document, from a simple email or blog post to an executive summary of 10 pages.

A good way to start developing your logic is by answering these questions:

- Why should I write this? What do I want the reader to do after reading it?
- What's the main point of my document – what are its key points?
- How will this help me achieve my goal (what am I trying to get across)?

In addition, being able to create documents that are free from errors shows your company you have attention to detail skills that may lead to other promotion opportunities in the future.

Key Pointers:

- Always proofread your work.
- Make sure you have the correct spelling and grammar.
- Use the spell checker in your word processing software to ensure that you've spelled things correctly. For example, if you're writing "I," it would be better if you wrote "I" instead of just writing out "i." This makes it easier for people to understand what they're reading as well as being more professional looking on paper (and in other places such as

LinkedIn profiles or resumes). It also helps avoid any potential confusion with other words like "it" which may be misused when used interchangeably with "I."

- Make sure that all punctuation marks are used appropriately throughout the document so that readers can easily follow along without having trouble understanding where each part belongs within sentences themselves; for example: use commas after every sentence except those ending sentences rather than periods because these types of punctuations help break up paragraphs more effectively than do spaces alone do otherwise might lead them down rabbit trails until finally finding their way back home again but then again maybe not always :)

Lastly, business writing is the foundation of all job applications. It's critical for both managers and employees to master this skill, as it will come in handy throughout your career. Having good writing skills can be helpful for:

- Managers who must communicate with their teams about projects, tasks and goals
- Clerks who must write up receipts or other customer communications after a transaction has been made

- Consultants who have to write proposals for clients' business needs

It's important for all professionals to understand how to write an effective memo or business letter, especially those in management or positions that deal with clients.

Memos and business letters are important tools in business communication. Memos are used to communicate information between co-workers, while letters can be used for communicating with clients, customers and suppliers. Both types of documents help you make connections with others through effective communication that is clear and concise.

In order to write a memo or letter that is effective, it's important to know how to use proper grammar and punctuation so that your message comes across clearly without being too formal or informal.

If you want your memos/letters read by someone else (such as an executive), then they need be easy-to-read; however if they're going straight into an email inbox then there shouldn't be any unnecessary fluff like run-on sentences or passive voice phrases like "was" instead of "are."

- You are expected to be a good writer. As a professional, you will often play an important role as an ambassador between two parties.
- You must be able to communicate effectively with clients and coworkers. As a business writer, you will also have many people in your life who depend on your ability to communicate clearly and effectively.
- Finally, if there are any supervisors or managers at work who oversee your activities—and hopefully they do—they may expect the same from themselves!

Written communication should be top-notch. It is not enough to have an engaging conversation with your boss or colleagues; you need to be able to write effectively as well. Business writing is an essential skill that will help you in the workplace and make your career more successful than it would otherwise be.

Business writing skills are necessary for all professionals, not just managers. If you want your company's culture to reflect an effective way of communicating with employees and customers alike, then business writing is one way that can help achieve this goal.

Strong business communication skills are critical for success in today's world of work.

Business writing is a skill that all employees need, no matter what their position or industry. Whether you're an entry-level intern, mid-level employee, or senior manager with years of experience under your belt—business communication skills are important for success in today's world of work.

Business writing is also critical for all levels of management. When communicating with colleagues and superiors alike, it helps to have an understanding of who they are as people and what they care about most professionally (and personally). If you don't know how someone thinks or feels when they read something written down on paper by someone else—then chances are good that this person won't want anything more than just another job description filled out by yours truly!

As you can see, there are many benefits of business writing. In fact, studies show that being able to communicate effectively is one of the most important skills you can have as a professional.

If you want to become more proficient at writing, then start by taking some time each week to practice!

Table 1.0 - Tone Guidelines for Business Writing:

Tone	Situational Use
Formal	Professional settings
Casual	Internal communications
Assertive	Negotiations and directives

10 Laws of Business Writing

For my first interview as a Blockleaders' writer, I wanted to get Jordan Gitterman to speak on every element of inspiration, direction, and conviction. I had known Jordan for quite some time now. We met on LinkedIn and I immediately noticed his thirst for challenging the status quo and getting things done. Read Interview here - simple input in your browser - https://www.blockleaders.io/leaders/jordan-gitterman-taking-on-world-hunger-and-global-parity-valuation-with-the-power-of-blockchain..

I believed he would make a great interviewee as he had a lot to share about his forays into the world of blockchain and Global Parity Valuation via his project, ItemBanc.

Mr. Gitterman is focused on developing cryptocurrencies, and blockchain technologies that have a positive social impact. He has over 30 years of business management and finance experience with a considerable amount of it in hard asset projects.

Item Banc's focus on addressing global poverty and hunger became Jordan's mission. Motivated by empathy and a desire to tackle systemic challenges, he sees technology as a tool to turn ideas into solutions. Item Banc's technology engine, designed for global parity valuation, captures data from basic human need goods exchanges organized by nation, using smart contracts.

Why Africa? Jordan strategically chose Africa, particularly Rwanda, recognizing the continent's pressing economic needs. With 54 countries trading in 56 different currencies, Africa faces inflation and a disconnect between economic performance and currency value. Item Banc aims to alleviate these challenges by reducing friction in trading and correcting misnomers in valuations.

As we concluded our conversation, Jordan shared his hopes for the future—a future where Item Banc's Global Parity Valuation Engine empowers communities worldwide. His vision includes spurring strong trade systems, delivering confidence, security, and freedom in currency-challenged communities, ultimately contributing to the growth of smart, productive economies. Jordan's journey from realtor to blockchain advocate exemplifies the transformative power of technology in addressing global challenges.

Drawing inspiration from Gitterman's story, we explore how effective writing captures the essence of change, translating it into a narrative that resonates with stakeholders. From real estate discontent to blockchain innovation, Gitterman's experience becomes a guide for crafting compelling business narratives that communicate evolution, vision, and purpose.

Graph 1.0 – Most Common Misused Words in Business Writing

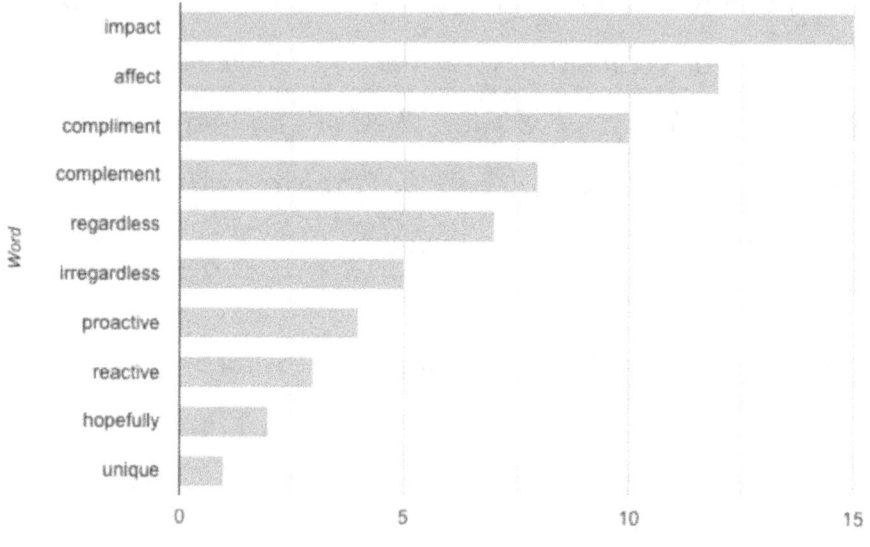

Most Common Misused Words in Business Writing

Frequency of Misuse

These business writing rules will help you craft interesting and authoritative business communication sentences. They are simply laws that seek to shape your world view of writing formal or slightly formal texts to colleagues, an employee, employer or a client. I must remind you that they are not a 1 vs 1 situation. Some laws are polar opposites of each other, and will require your personal discernment of understanding the situation when deciding to apply Law 1 or Law 10.

These guidelines apply to most types of business writing, not just electronic mail.

Law 1: Write more casually.

Don't try to sound smart all the time. Instead, write how you speak: read your content aloud to ensure it has a natural rhythm and flow. Simple language and phrase patterns should be used. Use the active voice instead of the passive voice more often. Address readers directly, using "I," "us," and "you" as needed.

Casual business conversations even in the most formal setting is not forbidden. It makes your texts more interesting and understandable.

Law 2- Be Distinct:

Be yourself, and let your writing reflect that. Often, business owners are concerned about making the appropriate impression, so they delete everything that makes them stand out from the material. This makes the writing monotonous. Your unique approach will be appreciated by your audience.

Effective business writing will attract more consumers and help you grow your business. Keep your focus on the style and let the result speak for itself.

Law 3- Say what you mean plainly:

Simple and informative corporate communication is essential. You want to communicate your important themes clearly, simply, and directly.

Simple language and sentence patterns, as well as brief paragraphs, should be used, but not at the expense of information. Take the effort to select accurate phrases to communicate your views. One longer, clear term that communicates exactly what you mean might be more instructive than numerous shorter ones.

Your readers aren't psychics. State the facts accurately and explain them; do not rely on innuendo and suggestion.

Edit and organize your language carefully to ensure that the important information shines out. Your writing should be factual and succinct, with no unnecessary information or diversion. Proofread thoroughly to avoid spelling and grammatical errors.

Law 4 : Be Genuine.

Maintain your integrity. People want and respond to sincerity and honesty. The more your material seems like it was written by a genuine person, the greater influence it will have on your readers. They'll think about it more and remember it better as a result.

Even when writing about business, write from the heart. Say what you think and believe what you think.

Tell the truth about what happened. When the reality is difficult to accept, look for and focus on the positives. Be as forthcoming as possible.

Know your audience and envision how your words will affect them. When you write with your readers in mind, it's frequently simpler to be true and honest.

Law 5: Use jargon and slang sparingly.

Except for those that you are convinced everyone in your target audience will understand, avoid utilizing corporate jargon, acronyms, and abbreviations. Complex jargon might make you (or your business) appear arrogant rather than authoritative. If they don't grasp it, it may alienate some readers by making them feel confused or alienated.

Similarly, except for popular terminology and idioms, avoid colloquialisms and slang. While they may make your business writing sound more casual, they may not be understood by everyone.

Law 6: Begin each phrase with And or But.

The old school rule about avoiding beginning a sentence with "And" or "But" (or However, Also, Or, because...) was always rubbish. Since the ninth century, this sentence structure has been employed in English. The rule stems from 17th century professors attempting to impose Latin grammatical norms on English.

Start with And, But, etc. if it helps you compose short, straightforward phrases. Just don't go overboard (or it becomes repetitive).

Law 7: Write Short paragraphs

You may have heard that a paragraph should have at least three sentences. Single-sentence paragraphs have long been appropriate in creative, casual, and corporate writing. Even more so now that the conventions of web writing are spilling over into print. Do it if it helps you add impact.

Law 8: Make use of contractions.

Many individuals believe that contractions (it's, don't, won't, etc.) should only be used in casual writing and so avoid using them in professional business writing.

Not so. Even in the most formal settings, individuals use contractions while speaking, and there's no reason why they shouldn't be written. These verb forms are learnt in the first year of learning English, whether you're a newborn learning your mother tongue or an adult non-native speaker. Use contractions if they help you maintain your tone of speech authentic and straightforward.

Law 8: Preposition to end a statement Conundrum.
Prepositions are words that connect a noun, verb, or adjective to a noun or pronoun, such as to, by, for, with, on, in, about, or at. They are usually, but not always, used before a noun or pronoun in a phrase or clause.

The widespread assumption that you should never conclude a sentence with a preposition derives from misinformed ancient professors. You CAN write "We finally received the package we had been waiting for," rather of "...the delivery for which we had been waiting."

Of course, you might alter that to "We received the long-awaited delivery." or "The items came."

Law 9: Split infinitives

You may have also learnt that you shouldn't insert words between "to" and a verb, as in "To confidently go…" or "Expect sales to more than double". Another ancient rule you may easily disregard. Avoiding split infinitives may result in uncomfortable phrases or even modify the meaning of the statement.

Law 10: Express yourself.

People have emotions even while they are at work and conducting business. When things don't go as planned, you may experience feelings of irritation or wrath. People's emotions may either help or impede productive business collaboration. In this post (input - https://fortifiedthinking.com/index.php/2023/11/06/how-to-forge-a-warriors-mentality/), check what it means to develop a warrior's mindset

Foundations of Business Writing

Understanding Your Audience

Effective business writing begins with a keen understanding of your audience. The ability to tailor your message to the specific needs, preferences, and expectations of your readers is fundamental to successful communication in the business world. In this chapter, we delve deep into the nuances of audience analysis and explore how it forms the bedrock of impactful business writing.

Identifying Your Audience

Before penning a single word, it's crucial to identify who your audience is. Whether you're composing an email, a report, or a proposal, the first step is recognizing the individuals who will be reading your document. Are they colleagues, clients, superiors, or a combination of these? What are their roles, interests, and levels of familiarity with the topic? The more precise your understanding, the more effectively you can tailor your communication to resonate with them.

Consider the following scenario: you're tasked with drafting a project proposal for a diverse audience that includes technical experts, financial analysts, and project managers. Each group has distinct

priorities and concerns. The technical experts may be interested in the feasibility of the project from a technical standpoint, while financial analysts would likely focus on budgetary considerations. Project managers might be more concerned with timelines and resource allocation. Recognizing these differences enables you to craft a proposal that addresses the unique needs of each segment, making your document more relevant and compelling.

Analyzing Audience Characteristics

Beyond basic identification, understanding your audience involves a deeper analysis of their characteristics. Factors such as age, educational background, cultural diversity, and professional experience can significantly influence how your message is received. For instance, a report intended for a team of seasoned professionals might use industry-specific terminology and assume a certain level of expertise. In contrast, if your audience includes individuals from different departments or varying levels of experience, a more straightforward and inclusive approach may be necessary.

Consider the language you use—jargon that's familiar to one group may be confusing or alienating to another. Strive for a balance that ensures your writing is accessible to all intended readers. This not only enhances comprehension but also fosters a sense of inclusivity, acknowledging and respecting the diversity within your audience.

Grasping Audience Expectations

Every reader approaches a document with certain expectations. Whether it's a formal report, a project update, or a casual email, your audience anticipates a certain tone, level of formality, and structure. Understanding and meeting these expectations is vital for effective communication.

For example, imagine you're composing an email to update your team on a project's progress. If your team is accustomed to concise, bulleted updates, providing a lengthy narrative might not align with their expectations. Conversely, if the situation demands a more detailed explanation, deviating from the norm without proper justification could lead to confusion or frustration.

To meet these expectations, consider past interactions, established communication norms within your organization, and the nature of the message itself. Adapting your writing style to align with these expectations ensures that your message is not only heard but also received in the manner intended.

Addressing Audience Needs

Ultimately, effective business writing goes beyond meeting expectations; it addresses the needs of the audience. What information are they seeking? What challenges are they facing? What action do you want them to take after reading your document?

Continuing with the project proposal example, your audience's needs may vary. While technical experts might require detailed specifications and feasibility analyses, financial analysts may be more interested in cost projections and return on investment. By anticipating and directly addressing these needs, your writing becomes purposeful and outcome-driven.

Consider incorporating a section in your document explicitly addressing potential questions or concerns your audience might have. This proactive approach not only demonstrates your thoroughness but also streamlines the communication process, making it easier for your audience to extract the information they need.

In conclusion, understanding your audience is the cornerstone of effective business writing. By identifying, analyzing, and addressing

the unique characteristics and expectations of your readers, you lay the groundwork for communication that is not only clear and concise but also relevant and impactful. As we sail through the subsequent chapters, this foundational knowledge will serve as a compass, guiding us toward writing that resonates with the diverse audience that defines the business landscape.

Defining Your Purpose

When it comes to business writing, clarity of purpose is paramount. Defining your purpose is akin to setting the sails before a voyage – it directs your writing, giving it purpose and ensuring that your message resonates with its intended audience. In this section, we explore the intricacies of crafting a clear and compelling purpose for your business documents, whether it's a report, a proposal, or a simple email.

The Significance of Purpose in Business Writing

Before delving into the practical aspects of defining your purpose, let's underscore why this step is so critical. Your purpose serves as the guiding star for your writing, influencing every decision from content selection to tone and style. Without a clearly defined purpose, your message risks becoming convoluted, meandering, or, worse, missing the mark altogether.

Consider a scenario where you're tasked with drafting a proposal for a new project. If your purpose is unclear or vague, your document may lack focus, making it challenging for readers to grasp the key objectives or benefits of the proposed initiative. On the other hand, a well-defined purpose, such as securing approval for project funding or outlining the potential return on investment, provides a clear roadmap for your writing, ensuring that every section contributes meaningfully to achieving your goals.

Identifying Your Objectives

The first step in defining your purpose is identifying your objectives. What do you aim to achieve with your business writing? Are you informing, persuading, instructing, or a combination of these? Each objective requires a different approach, and your writing must be tailored accordingly.

Let's take the example of a business report. If your objective is to inform stakeholders about the performance of a recently implemented strategy, your writing will focus on presenting facts, data, and outcomes. On the other hand, if the goal is to persuade investors to support a new initiative, your writing will emphasize the potential benefits, addressing concerns, and making a compelling case for investment.

By clearly articulating your objectives, you not only provide direction to your writing but also help your audience understand the purpose of your communication from the outset.

Tailoring Your Message to Your Purpose

Once your objectives are established, the next step is tailoring your message to align seamlessly with your purpose. Consider the tone, style, and level of formality that best suit your objectives and audience.

For instance, if your purpose is to instruct employees on a new company policy, a clear and authoritative tone may be appropriate. On the other hand, if you're announcing a company-wide achievement, a celebratory and appreciative tone might be more fitting.

In addition to tone, consider the level of detail required to fulfill your purpose. A proposal seeking approval for a significant project might demand an in-depth analysis of costs, benefits, and risks. In contrast, a brief status update may only require key highlights and outcomes.

Understanding Your Audience's Needs in Relation to Your Purpose

While we explored audience needs in the previous section, it's crucial to revisit this concept in the context of defining your purpose. Your purpose should align with and address the specific needs of your audience.

Going back to the project proposal example, if your purpose is to secure funding, your writing should explicitly address the financial considerations that matter to your audience. What is the expected return on investment? How does the proposed project align with the organization's strategic goals? By framing your purpose in relation to your audience's needs, you create a more compelling and relevant message.

Consider conducting a brief audience analysis to ensure that your defined purpose resonates with your readers. What are their priorities? What information are they seeking? By aligning your purpose with their needs, you increase the likelihood of engagement and understanding.

Crafting a Purpose Statement

To crystallize your purpose, consider crafting a purpose statement. This concise declaration, usually placed near the beginning of your document, clearly communicates the intent of your writing. It serves as a beacon, guiding your readers and preparing them for the content that follows.

A purpose statement for a project proposal seeking funding could be: "This proposal aims to secure financial support for [Project Name] by presenting a comprehensive analysis of its anticipated benefits, costs, and alignment with the company's strategic objectives."

For a report informing stakeholders about a new marketing strategy, the purpose statement might be: "This report seeks to inform stakeholders about the successful implementation of the [Marketing Strategy], highlighting key performance indicators, outcomes, and future implications."

By encapsulating your purpose in a succinct statement, you provide a roadmap for your readers, signaling what to expect and why your message is important.

Revisiting and Refining Your Purpose

The process of defining your purpose is not a one-time endeavor; it's an iterative and dynamic aspect of business writing. As you progress through the writing process, continually revisit and refine your purpose. Does each section of your document align with your stated objectives? Is the tone consistent with your purpose statement? Regularly reassessing and adjusting ensures that your writing remains focused and purposeful.

Consider soliciting feedback from colleagues or peers. A fresh perspective can reveal areas where your purpose may be unclear or where adjustments could enhance the impact of your message.

In conclusion, defining your purpose is a foundational step in effective business writing. By identifying objectives, tailoring your message, aligning with audience needs, crafting a purpose statement, and revisiting your purpose throughout the writing process, you lay the groundwork for communication that is not only clear and purposeful but also resonates with your audience. As we progress, remember that purpose is the anchor that keeps your business writing grounded and impactful.

Common Types of Business Documents

In the dynamic landscape of business communication, various document types serve distinct purposes, each demanding a tailored approach to convey information effectively. We will explore the intricacies of crafting three common types of business documents: Emails and Memos, Reports and Proposals, and Business Letters. Understanding the conventions, structures, and best practices for each document type empowers you to communicate with precision and impact.

a. Emails and Memos

Emails and memos are the workhorses of day-to-day business communication, providing quick and efficient means to convey information, coordinate activities, and make decisions. Mastering the art of crafting effective emails and memos is essential for maintaining clear and concise communication within an organization. Let's highlight key elements, shall we?

Subject Line Clarity

The subject line serves as the gateway to your email or memo. A clear and concise subject line not only grabs the recipient's attention but also conveys the main purpose of the communication. Whether it's a project update, a meeting request, or a decision-making memo, a well-crafted subject line sets the tone for what follows.

Consider the difference between a vague subject line like "Meeting" and a specific one such as "Project Kickoff Meeting: Agenda and Action Items." The latter provides clarity and context, helping recipients prioritize and engage with the content.

Concise and Focused Content

Effective emails and memos are characterized by brevity and focus. In the fast-paced business environment, recipients appreciate communication that gets straight to the point. Begin with a brief introduction, followed by the main content, and conclude with a clear call to action or next steps.

Avoid unnecessary details or tangential information. Each paragraph should contribute to the central message, enhancing comprehension and reducing the risk of information overload.

Professional Tone in Digital Communication

While the tone in emails and memos can vary based on the nature of the message and the relationship with the recipient, maintaining a professional tone is crucial. Even in a more casual context, professionalism contributes to clarity and fosters a positive impression.

Be mindful of language choice, grammar, and formatting. Consider your audience and the formality expectations within your organization. Striking the right balance between friendliness and professionalism ensures that your digital communication aligns with organizational norms.

Effective Use of Attachments and Links

Attachments and links can enhance the effectiveness of emails and memos, providing additional context or supporting documentation. However, their use should be strategic. Clearly indicate the purpose of attachments or links in the body of the email, and ensure that they are relevant to the main message.

When attaching files, consider using standardized file naming conventions and formats to facilitate easy access and understanding. Be cautious with large attachments, as they can impact email deliverability and create inconvenience for recipients.

Addressing Recipients and Including Clear Calls to Action

Personalization and clear calls to action contribute to the effectiveness of emails and memos. Address recipients by name whenever possible, and use direct language to convey expectations. Clearly articulate what action, if any, is required from the recipient and include deadlines if applicable.

For example, instead of a vague request like "Let me know your thoughts," specify the desired action with a direct call to action such as "Please provide your feedback on the proposed budget by [date]."

b. Reports and Proposals

Reports and proposals are comprehensive documents designed to inform, analyze, and persuade. Whether it's a project report, a financial analysis, or a business proposal, mastering the conventions of reports and proposals is essential for conveying complex information in a structured and compelling manner. The key elements include:

Clear Structure and Organization

The structure of reports and proposals plays a pivotal role in facilitating understanding. Begin with a clear introduction that outlines the purpose and scope of the document. Follow with well-defined sections, each addressing specific aspects of the topic. Common sections include executive summary, methodology, findings, analysis, recommendations, and conclusion.

Use headings and subheadings to guide the reader through the document. A well-organized structure enhances readability and helps readers locate information efficiently.

Executive Summary as a Snapshot

The executive summary serves as a snapshot of the entire report or proposal. Crafted succinctly, it provides a brief overview of the key findings, recommendations, and conclusions. The executive summary is often the first section that busy executives or decision-makers read, influencing their decision to delve deeper into the document.

Ensure that the executive summary captures the essence of the document, highlighting the most critical information. Despite its brevity, it should convey a comprehensive understanding of the document's key points.

Data Presentation and Visualization

Reports and proposals often involve presenting data and analysis. Effective data presentation is not just about including numbers but also about making the data accessible and understandable for the reader. Consider using charts, graphs, and tables to visually represent complex information.

Choose visualizations that align with the nature of the data. For example, a bar chart might be suitable for comparing quantities, while a line chart could illustrate trends over time. Clearly label and explain visual elements to ensure their interpretation aligns with your intended message.

Analytical and Interpretative Writing

Analysis and interpretation are core elements of reports and proposals. Moving beyond presenting raw data, your writing should provide insights and interpretations that guide the reader toward understanding the implications of the information presented.

Use clear and concise language to explain your analysis. Avoid assumptions and provide context for your interpretations. When proposing recommendations, tie them directly to your analysis, demonstrating a logical and evidence-based approach.

Persuasive Language and Tone

In proposals, persuasive language is key to influencing decision-makers. Craft your language to emphasize the benefits of your proposal and address potential concerns. Use confident and assertive language without being overly aggressive.

Consider the difference between a hesitant statement like "This proposal might improve efficiency" and a more persuasive one such as "This proposal will significantly enhance efficiency by streamlining processes and reducing turnaround time."

Tailoring Language to Your Audience

Understanding your audience is crucial in crafting reports and proposals. Tailor your language to the level of familiarity your audience has with the subject matter. Avoid unnecessary jargon, and provide explanations for technical terms when needed. Consider the perspectives and priorities of your audience. For example, a proposal presented to a finance team might emphasize cost savings and return on investment, while a proposal for a marketing initiative might highlight brand impact and audience engagement.

c. Business Letters

Business letters, though less common in the age of digital communication, maintain relevance for formal communication with external entities, such as clients, partners, or government agencies. Understanding the conventions of business letters ensures that your written correspondence maintains a professional and polished appearance. Key ingredients include:

Formal Salutations and Closings

The salutation and closing of a business letter set the tone for the entire communication. Use formal salutations such as "Dear Mr. Smith" or

"To Whom It May Concern" based on the level of familiarity with the recipient. Similarly, choose closings that reflect professionalism, such as "Sincerely" or "Yours faithfully."

Ensure that the salutation and closing align with the formality expectations of your organization and the nature of the correspondence.

Addressing the Recipient and Including Contact Information

Clearly address the recipient in the business letter, including their full name and appropriate title. If you are unsure about the recipient's title, it's advisable to conduct a brief research or inquiry to ensure accuracy. Including the recipient's contact information, such as their address or reference number, can facilitate efficient processing and response.

For example, a well-constructed address might read: "Ms. Emily Johnson, Director of Client Services, XYZ Corporation, 123 Main Street, Cityville, State, Zip Code."

Concise and Polished Language

Business letters should embody a level of formality and professionalism. Choose language that is clear, concise, and polished. Avoid overly complex sentences and strive for clarity in conveying your message.

Consider the purpose of your letter. If you are making a request, state it directly and provide any necessary details. If you are conveying information, present it logically and in a manner that aligns with the expectations of a formal letter.

Specific and Purposeful Content

Ensure that the content of your business letter is specific and purposeful. Clearly state the reason for your communication in the opening paragraphs. If you are making a request, specify the details and any relevant deadlines. If you are providing information, ensure it is comprehensive and addresses the key points.

For instance, a business letter requesting a meeting might state: "I am writing to request a meeting with you to discuss the implementation of the new marketing strategy. I propose a meeting date of [specific date] at [specific time]."

Addressing Concerns and Offering Solutions

If your business letter addresses a concern or problem, adopt a constructive and solution-oriented approach. Clearly articulate the issue, provide any relevant context, and propose potential solutions. Demonstrating a proactive mindset and a willingness to collaborate enhances the effectiveness of your letter.

For instance, a letter addressing a service issue might include: "I am writing to bring to your attention a recent discrepancy in the invoicing process. To resolve this matter, I suggest a thorough review of the billing records and a discussion to implement corrective measures."

Formal Tone and Language Choice

Maintain a formal tone throughout your business letter. Even if the recipient is known to you, business letters call for a level of formality that aligns with professional standards. Choose words and phrases carefully, ensuring that they convey respect and professionalism.

For example, instead of using informal language like "Hey" or "Hi," opt for more formal salutations such as "Dear" or "Greetings."

Enclosures and Additional Documentation

If your business letter includes enclosures or additional documentation, clearly mention them in the body of the letter. This ensures that the recipient is aware of any supplementary materials and can refer to them as needed.

For instance, a letter accompanying a report might state: "Enclosed, please find the detailed report on the market analysis for your review. I believe the findings will be instrumental in our upcoming strategy discussions."

Formatting and Professional Appearance

The formatting of a business letter contributes to its professional appearance. Use a standard business letter format, including your contact information, the date, the recipient's address, a formal salutation, the body of the letter, a formal closing, and your signature. Consistency in formatting across all business letters enhances a professional and organized image.

Proofreading for Accuracy and Tone

Before finalizing and sending a business letter, conduct a thorough proofreading. Check for accuracy in names, addresses, and any other details. Ensure that the tone is consistent with the formality expected in a business context.

Pay attention to grammar, spelling, and punctuation. A well-proofread letter enhances your professional image and reduces the likelihood of miscommunication.

Finally…

The skills developed in mastering business document writing are transferable across various professional contexts. Whether you are communicating internally within your organization or externally with clients and partners, the principles outlined in this chapter will serve as valuable tools in your business writing toolkit. As we proceed, these foundational skills will continue to inform and elevate your business writing endeavors.

Effective Communication in the Digital Age

Effective communication in the digital age is essential for success. This chapter explores the intricacies of utilizing digital communication platforms, optimizing virtual meetings, and leveraging collaborative tools. As technology continues to reshape the way we interact, mastering digital communication skills becomes a key competency for professionals in diverse fields.

Digital Communication Platforms

Digital communication platforms have become integral to modern business interactions. Whether it's email, instant messaging, or collaborative tools, understanding how to explore and leverage these platforms is crucial for effective communication.

Email Etiquette in the Digital Era

Email remains a primary mode of business communication, and adhering to email etiquette is essential. In the digital era, where inboxes can quickly become overwhelming, efficient communication is key.

Consider the following principles:

Clear and Concise Subject Lines: Craft subject lines that provide a clear indication of the email's content.

Structured and Organized Content: Use paragraphs and bullet points to break up text, making your email easy to read.

Appropriate Tone: Maintain a professional tone and avoid misinterpretation by choosing words carefully.

Timely Responses: Aim to respond to emails promptly, acknowledging receipt or providing necessary information.

Instant Messaging and Collaboration Platforms

Instant messaging and collaboration platforms, such as Slack or Microsoft Teams, have transformed real-time communication in the workplace. To maximize their effectiveness:

Use Clear and Direct Messaging: Be concise and to the point in instant messages, while still maintaining professionalism.

Utilize Channels Effectively: Organize conversations into relevant channels to streamline communication and avoid clutter.

Respect Working Hours: Be mindful of colleagues' working hours when sending non-urgent messages to promote a healthy work-life balance.

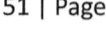

Optimizing Virtual Meetings

Virtual meetings have become commonplace, offering flexibility but also presenting unique challenges. Mastering the art of virtual meetings enhances collaboration and ensures productive communication.

Preparation and Agenda Setting

Effective virtual meetings begin with thorough preparation. Consider:

Setting Clear Objectives: Define the purpose of the meeting and communicate it in advance.

Creating an Agenda: Share a detailed agenda outlining topics, presenters, and expected outcomes.

Technical Checks: Ensure all participants are familiar with the meeting platform and have tested their audio and video setups.

Engaging Virtual Participants

Keeping participants engaged in a virtual setting requires deliberate efforts:

Encourage Participation: Actively involve participants through questions, polls, or breakout discussions.

Visual Engagement: Incorporate visuals, such as slides or shared documents, to maintain interest.

Manage Meeting Length: Keep virtual meetings concise and focused to prevent participant fatigue.

Effective Communication and Etiquette

Maintaining effective communication etiquette is crucial in virtual meetings:

Clear Communication: Speak clearly and concisely, avoiding jargon or overly technical language.

Active Listening: Foster a culture of active listening by encouraging participants to provide input and ask questions.

Camera Presence: When on video, maintain eye contact and project a professional appearance.

Handling Technical Challenges

Technical issues are inevitable in virtual meetings. Be prepared to troubleshoot common challenges:

Backup Plans: Have contingency plans in case of platform issues or disruptions.

Technical Support: Assign someone to provide technical support during the meeting.

Recording Meetings: Record meetings for participants who may encounter technical difficulties or for future reference.

Leveraging Collaborative Tools

Collaborative tools enhance teamwork and streamline communication. Understanding how to leverage these tools optimally contributes to a more efficient and interconnected work environment.

Document Collaboration Platforms

Platforms like Google Workspace, Microsoft 365, or Dropbox facilitate seamless document collaboration. Tips for effective use include:

Version Control: Clearly label document versions and establish version control practices.

Real-Time Editing: Leverage real-time editing features to enhance collaboration during virtual meetings.

Commenting and Feedback: Use commenting features for feedback and suggestions on shared documents.

Project Management Tools

Project management tools, such as Trello, Asana, or Jira, aid in organizing and tracking tasks. Optimize their use by:

Task Assignment: Clearly assign tasks to team members, specifying deadlines and expectations.

Progress Tracking: Regularly update task statuses and use visual dashboards to monitor overall project progress.

Communication Integration: Integrate communication features within project management tools for seamless collaboration.

Video Conferencing Platforms

Video conferencing platforms, like Zoom or Microsoft Teams, facilitate face-to-face virtual interactions. Ensure optimal usage by:

Professional Backgrounds: Choose professional and non-distracting backgrounds during video calls.

Meeting Recording: Record important meetings for reference or for participants who couldn't attend.

Screen Sharing: Effectively use screen-sharing features to present information or collaborate on documents.

Security and Privacy Considerations

With the increasing reliance on digital tools, prioritize security and privacy:

Secure Access: Implement secure access controls and authentication measures for collaborative tools.

Data Encryption: Ensure that data transmitted and stored within collaborative platforms is encrypted.

Privacy Policies: Familiarize yourself with the privacy policies of the tools you use and communicate them to your team.

As we traverse the digital communication landscape, the principles of clarity, professionalism, and adaptability remain paramount. Mastery of digital communication platforms, virtual meetings, and collaborative tools empowers professionals to thrive in the contemporary business environment.

Remember that effective communication in the digital age is not just about technology; it's about leveraging these tools to enhance human connection, collaboration, and productivity. The skills developed in this chapter will serve you well as you embrace the evolving nature of digital communication in your professional journey.

Unbridling Your Creativity

In my book "Creative Thinking for Leaders and Dreamers', I delved deep into the world of innovative thought processes, urging leaders to embrace their inner dreamers. The lessons from that book are seamlessly interwoven with the principles I'm about to unveil in this chapter. Much like the symbiotic relationship between creativity and effective leadership, the art of business writing thrives on a foundation of originality and inventive expression.

Effective business writing begins with thoughtful planning. This chapter explores pre-writing strategies, techniques for organizing your thoughts, and the creation of outlines to ensure clarity and coherence in your written communication.

Pre-writing Strategies

Pre-writing is the initial phase of the writing process where you brainstorm, gather ideas, and lay the foundation for your document.

Understanding Your Purpose and Audience

Before putting pen to paper, define the purpose of your writing and identify your target audience:

Purpose Clarity: Clearly articulate the main goal or objective of your communication.

Audience Analysis: Understand the characteristics, needs, and expectations of your audience.

Brainstorming and Mind Mapping

Engage in brainstorming and mind mapping to generate ideas and organize your thoughts:

Free-Flow Ideation: Allow ideas to flow without immediate judgment to encourage creativity.

Mind Maps: Create visual representations of connections between ideas to enhance understanding.

Research and Information Gathering

Conduct thorough research and gather relevant information to support your writing:

Credible Sources: Utilize reliable sources to enhance the credibility of your content.

Data Collection: Gather data, statistics, or examples that reinforce your key points.

Organizing Your Thoughts

Once you have a pool of ideas, it's essential to organize them in a coherent manner to effectively convey your message.

Logical Sequence

Organize your thoughts in a logical sequence that aligns with the natural flow of information:

Chronological Order: Arrange information based on a timeline or sequence of events.
Order of Importance: Prioritize key points based on their significance to the main message.

Grouping Related Ideas

Group related ideas and concepts to create cohesive sections within your document:

Thematic Grouping: Group ideas based on common themes or topics.

Subheadings: Use subheadings to guide readers and signal transitions between different sections.

Thesis Statement or Main Message

Craft a clear thesis statement or main message that encapsulates the core idea of your communication:

Central Focus: Clearly express the main point or argument you aim to convey.

Guiding Element: Use the thesis statement as a guide for maintaining focus throughout your writing.

Creating Outlines for Clarity

Outlining serves as a roadmap for your writing, providing structure and clarity to your thoughts.

Hierarchical Structure

Use a hierarchical structure to organize ideas in a clear and easily understandable manner:

Main Points and Subpoints: Distinguish between primary and supporting ideas.

Parallel Structure: Maintain consistency in the structure of each outline level for coherence.

Annotated Outlines

Consider using annotated outlines that include brief notes or explanations for each section:

Content Notes: Provide additional context or details that support each outlined point.

Transition Notes: Include notes on how each section connects to the next for smoother transitions.

Flexibility and Adaptability

Keep your outline flexible to accommodate changes as your writing progresses:

Iterative Process: Understand that outlining is an iterative process that may evolve as you delve deeper into your writing.

Open to Revision: Be open to revising and adjusting your outline to enhance overall coherence.

Conclusively,

The planning phase is the bedrock of successful business writing. By employing pre-writing strategies, organizing your thoughts logically, and creating clear outlines, you set the stage for a writing process that is focused, coherent, and purposeful.

As you embark on your business writing journey, remember that the investment in careful planning pays dividends in the form of well-structured, impactful, and reader-friendly documents. The time and effort dedicated to the planning phase lay the groundwork for the success of your written communication in various professional contexts.

Bringing in Visual Appeal

In the realm of business writing, the visual appeal of documents plays a pivotal role in capturing and maintaining the reader's attention. This chapter explores strategies for incorporating graphics, optimizing formatting for readability, and designing effective visual elements to elevate the overall visual appeal of your business documents.

Incorporating Graphics and Images

Visual elements, such as graphics and images, are potent tools for conveying information and making your business documents visually engaging.

Selecting Relevant Graphics

Choosing the right graphics is essential for conveying information effectively:

Relevance to Content: Ensure that graphics directly support and enhance the content of the document.

Clarity of Message: Select graphics that succinctly convey the intended message without causing confusion.

Consistency in Style: Maintain a consistent style for graphics to create a cohesive visual experience.

Customizing Charts and Graphs

Charts and graphs are valuable for presenting data and trends. Customize them for clarity:

Appropriate Chart Type: Select the chart type that best represents the data, whether it's a bar chart, pie chart, or line graph.

Color Coding: Use color strategically to differentiate data points and enhance visual comprehension.

Descriptive Labels: Include clear and concise labels for axes and data points to aid interpretation.

Incorporating High-Quality Images

High-quality images contribute to the professional look of your documents:

Resolution and Clarity: Ensure images are high-resolution and clear, avoiding pixelation.

Consistent Theme: Maintain a consistent visual theme across images for a polished and cohesive appearance.

Proper Placement: Position images strategically to complement the flow of the content.

Using Formatting for Readability

Formatting is a powerful tool for enhancing the readability of business documents and ensuring that the information is easily digestible.

Consistent Font Usage

The choice and consistency of fonts impact the overall readability:

Font Selection: Choose clear and professional fonts that are easy to read.

Consistent Typeface: Maintain a consistent typeface throughout the document for a polished look.

Font Hierarchy: Use font sizes and styles to create a hierarchy that guides the reader through the content.

Strategic Use of Headings and Subheadings

Headings and subheadings help organize information and improve document navigation:

Clear Hierarchy: Establish a clear hierarchy of headings to convey the structure of the document.

Descriptive Headings: Craft headings that provide a snapshot of the content beneath them.

Consistent Formatting: Maintain consistent formatting for all headings to create visual harmony.

Utilizing Bulleted and Numbered Lists

Bulleted and numbered lists enhance content organization and readability:

Highlighting Key Points: Use lists to emphasize key information and make it stand out.

Parallel Structure: Ensure consistency in structure for items in lists to enhance readability.

Avoiding Overuse: Use lists judiciously to maintain the flow of the narrative.

Designing Effective Visual Elements

Beyond text and graphics, thoughtful design choices contribute to the overall effectiveness of your business documents.

White Space Management

Appropriate use of white space improves document clarity and prevents visual clutter:

Balancing Elements: Ensure a balanced distribution of text, graphics, and white space for visual harmony.

Facilitating Scanning: Use white space to guide the reader's eye and facilitate easy scanning of the document.

Emphasizing Key Content: Surround key content with white space to draw attention to critical information.

Color Palette Selection

A well-chosen color palette enhances visual appeal and reinforces branding:

Brand Consistency: Use colors that align with your brand identity to maintain a consistent visual image.

Contrast for Emphasis: Employ color contrast to highlight important elements and create visual interest.

Accessibility Considerations: Ensure color choices consider accessibility standards for diverse audiences.

Callouts and Text Boxes

Callouts and text boxes draw attention to specific information:

Highlighting Key Information: Use callouts to emphasize important points or provide additional context.

Clear Separation: Ensure text boxes create a clear separation from the main content for visual clarity.

Consistent Styling: Maintain a consistent style for callouts to enhance overall document coherence.

Captions and Annotations

Captions and annotations provide context and clarification for visuals:

Informative Captions: Craft captions that succinctly explain the relevance of visuals to the text.

Strategic Annotations: Use annotations strategically to provide additional details or insights.

Alignment with Visuals: Ensure that captions and annotations are positioned appropriately relative to the corresponding visuals.

In the dynamic landscape of business communication, the visual appeal of your documents significantly influences how information is received and understood. By incorporating relevant graphics, optimizing formatting for readability, and designing effective visual elements, you enhance the overall impact of your business writing.

As you apply the principles outlined in this chapter, remember that visual appeal is not a mere aesthetic consideration; it is a key factor in conveying professionalism and ensuring that your message resonates with your audience. Whether you are creating reports, proposals, or presentations, the strategic use of visuals and formatting will set your business documents apart in a crowded and competitive landscape.

Interlude

Let me ask you a question... What is your story?

I mean...

Do you or your company have a story? How did you come to where you are now, and why did you start your business?

We become accustomed to "pros" and others preaching to us that no one cares about us and is just interested in themselves.

Let's get started on your story.

Here's something I thought you would be interested in...

On one of my websites, I was checking at Google Analytics (basically page views, what people looked at and how long they were on my site). Over 75% of new visitors to my site viewed the page that talked about my journey.

Guess how many new people came to my testimonial page?

Barely 20%.

This indicates that more individuals were interested in learning about me rather than the results I produced for clients. Now, outcomes and proof are everything.

But here's the thing...

Your story has the potential to be quite powerful.

If you didn't think your tale was important or if you didn't know how to produce or tell your story, you're in luck. Why? Because I'm going to offer you some fast advice on how to start crafting your narrative and telling others about it.

However, first...

Want to know what you can add to your emails, sales letters, or any other sales communication to increase the number of people who read it?

Something that will keep your prospect flowing smoothly from one phrase to the next.

What exactly is it?

We're talking about the same subject. You're in for a treat right now if you haven't discovered this or tried utilizing tales for yourself. Including a narrative or storY in your communications might be an excellent approach to pull people in. Plus... A good tale may easily market your product for you.

There's also a really basic and straightforward approach to boost the likelihood of someone reading a lot more of your message and tale. I'll get to it in a moment, but first, let's discuss why tales are wonderful for selling or discussing your product, service, or business.

- Stories may be used to promote products or ideas.
- Stories may be used to both entertain and educate.

Here's an excellent example...Guess what the world's most renowned book is. The Holy Bible. It's jam-packed with tales. Some of the most successful and well-known advertisements of all time featured tales. The "most successful mail order ad of the twentieth century" was written by a copywriter named John Caples.

The title was(Paraphrased)...

"When I sat down at the piano, everybody laughed, but when I started playing... " A part of you wants to see the underdog triumph."

This title grabs your attention emotionally. You're curious about what happens and whether he freaks out or defeats the bullies. Does he perform well or fall flat on his face? They might have just spoken about music tuition in this ad, but the tale twists on another music product.

In other words, you enter into the tale, which is actually the advertisement. The tale handles the majority of the heavy work and selling for you.

To be precise...People are constantly interested in good stories.

We have loved and listened to stories since we were little. Even as adults, you may be sucked into a wild or entertaining narrative when at a family function or party.

Maybe your friend contacted you and gave you the most amusing or entertaining tale you've heard all day? Perhaps your spouse or wife just told you the "horror story" from work, or a bizarre occurrence involving a pal and the current gossip?

What I mean is... Stories may not only increase people's interest in your sales message, but they can also... As previously said, stories handle the "heavy lifting" of your sales message or aim.

CHAPTER 2 –

EMAIL

WRITING FOR

JOBS AND

EVENTS

Your 10 Markers

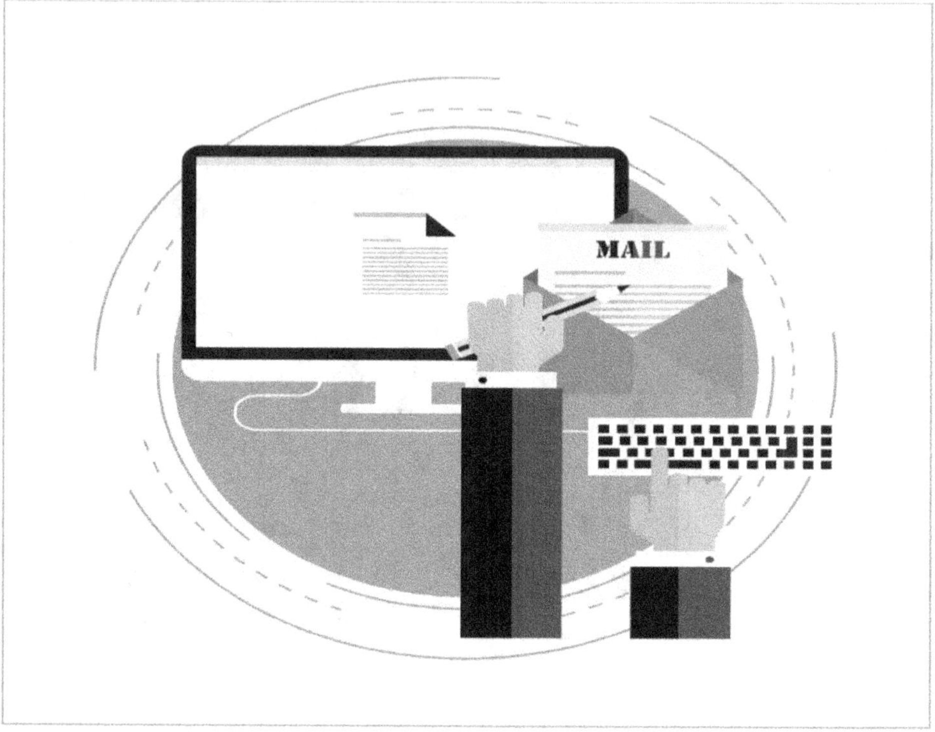

Let me share the inspiring journey of my friend and colleague, Nicholas Godwin, a prolific content creator who has left an indelible mark in the tech industry. Before his meteoric rise, Nicholas toiled in the trenches of a content mill research company, feeling the stagnation of his career. Determined to break free from the monotony, he embarked on a journey of self-improvement and rebranding.

Nicholas decided to upskill, honing his technical writing prowess, and soon found himself crafting content for industry giants like Bluehost,

Coursera, Copyscape, and Grammarly. His pivotal moment came when he ventured into entrepreneurship, establishing an agency that quickly soared to grossing an impressive 25-50k USD per month.

The road to success wasn't paved with ease. Nicholas, armed with tenacity, embraced a relentless approach to email pitching for jobs and contracts. In a testament to his perseverance, he famously sent over 100 applications before receiving his first response. This breakthrough became the catalyst for his transformation.

Since that monumental breakthrough, Nicholas has become a beacon of insight in the industry. Having explored the challenges, he discerns what works and what doesn't, offering invaluable expertise to those following in his footsteps. His journey is a testament to the boundless possibilities that arise when one combines skill development with unwavering determination. Nicholas Godwin not only achieved more than he envisaged but also continues to inspire others with his remarkable story of resilience and success.

Your job search starts with an email. It's one of the most common ways to communicate with potential employers and clients, so it's important that your resume, cover letter and other materials are written in a professional manner.

But when it comes down to it, there are a lot of things that can go wrong with any job application by a job seeker (and hiring managers don't have time to figure them out). So here are some tips for making sure that your next move into the world of employment doesn't fall flat on its face:

Email is one of the most common ways to communicate with potential clients and employers. It's also a great way to stay in touch with friends and family, as well as your dentist, pet sitter and more! It is an easy way to reach out when you don't want to call or knock on someone's door. You can send emails that are informal and conversational without having them feel like they're being ignored— but if you need something urgent (or important), emailing becomes much more formalized than calling someone up on their phone would be.

You can write a professional email that includes all the information your prospective employer needs to know about you.

Here are some tips for writing an effective email that includes everything you need to know about yourself, your resume and backup material:

- Don't write in first person. It feels too personal and can be perceived as a threat if you are applying for a job or event where the employer has met or interviewed other candidates in the past.

- Don't use slang words or acronyms unless they are part of your daily vocabulary or have been used by others around you (e.g., "I'll get back with ya"). If possible, try using these expressions in a different context before sending them out on paper so that no one gets confused!

- Avoid profanity when writing emails because this will make people think less of your professionalism; however, there may be situations where this is warranted (e.g., when talking about certain topics). If possible, avoid cursing altogether unless absolutely necessary—it makes us all look bad! We've already discussed how important it is not to send unsolicited material via email; keep this rule at heart when composing your messages as well."

- Use the right terminology and tone of voice for your job search.

- When writing your email, you want to be sure that it is clear and easily understood. You also want to make sure that the tone of your message is appropriate for the job posting.

- Use friendly language: Do not use a formal tone when writing an email application; instead, use language that focuses on what makes you stand out as a candidate. For example, if someone asks for examples of work experience, explain why their company would benefit from hiring someone with these skills and experiences—don't just say "I've worked at X Company" or "I've been working in this field since I was 16." Instead explain how those experiences relate specifically to what they're looking for in an applicant (e.g., "My previous experience includes..."). This will help them identify themselves as having similar interests/goals with yours!

- Be concise: In order for readers' attention span not get too short after reading just one line (or paragraph), try including fewer words per sentence than usual--this helps keep things interesting while still being able to convey everything necessary within each one! For example: "Hello," instead of hello everyone!"

- Include relevant information in your email subject line. Your subject line is the first thing that a recipient will see when they open your email. It should be short and to the point, so you want to make sure it's relevant to the content of your message. You can use up to 60 characters for your subject line, but don't go over 60 characters because that makes it harder for people on their phones or computers (and even some desktop computers) to read.

- When writing out potential email subjects in advance before sending them out, think about what kinds of emails have worked well for other professionals in similar situations as yours—and try not just doing what they did but also adding something unique! If there's an event happening soon after sending this email (e.g., Job Fair or Conference), consider giving some extra information about why we should attend: "Attending this conference will give us access" or "Attending this conference will allow us" etc..."

- Don't send hard-to-read attachments in an email.

- Sending large, complex and/or overly-detailed attachments can be a big turnoff. Don't send hard-to-read attachments in an email.

- It's also important to remember that if you're sending a resume, don't include any of the same information on the resume itself (like salary history). If they have access to your resume, they'll have access to all of the info there too!

- Hire an expert to help you craft an impeccable resume, cover letter and more. You're probably wondering how hiring a professional can benefit you. The answer is simple: they will make sure that your job application stands out from the crowd. They will also make sure that your resume gets read by people who matter in your field of interest, and they will teach you how to write a winning cover letter when applying for jobs or events like this one. This means more chances of getting hired!

How do I find someone who can help me with these tasks?

There are many websites out there where job seekers post their resumes and cover letters so other people can learn from them or even hire them directly if they want someone specific doing what needs doing (or writing). Look at some of these sites: Glassdoor , LinkedIn ,

Monster (for professionals) and Indeed (for those seeking employment).

When it comes down to it, there are a lot of things that can go wrong with any job application by a job seeker, and hiring managers don't have time to figure them out (or care!). But if you keep track of these mistakes (and don't make them!), you'll be well on your way to landing that dream job or internship!

First off: make sure your email subject line is relevant. Don't just type "Application" into the subject line—that's not what they want to see when they open their inboxes every day! The best thing about sending emails is that there's no limit on length; so long as it fits within the character count of most mail programs, you can write whatever makes sense for each situation.

To give an example: if I were applying for something like "job opening at XYZ Company" then I might use something like "XYZ Company Job Application." But if I was applying for an intern position at XYZ Company then my subject line would probably be different since most people wouldn't want everyone who applies knowing exactly what company they're applying too (even though those types of positions are usually advertised publicly).

So there you have it! If you follow these tips, your email should be well on its way to being a polished and professional job application.

Accepting Invites

Email Sample 1: Accepting a Job Interview Invitation

Subject: RE: Invitation to Job Interview at ABC Company

Dear [Hiring Manager's Name],

Thank you for considering my application for the position of [Job Title] at ABC Company. I'm excited to accept your invitation for a job interview on [Date] at [Time] at your office. I look forward to discussing my qualifications and learning more about the role and the company.

Please let me know if there's anything I should prepare for the interview or if there are any additional documents you require from me. I'm available for any further questions or clarification before the interview. Thank you again for the opportunity, and I look forward to meeting you soon.

Best regards,

[Your Name]

Email Sample 2: Accepting a Job Offer

Subject: Acceptance of Job Offer at XYZ Company

Dear [Hiring Manager's Name],

Thank you for offering me the position of [Job Title] at XYZ Company. I'm thrilled to accept your job offer and excited to join the team.

I appreciate your confidence in my abilities and look forward to contributing to the company's success. Please let me know if there are

any next steps I should take before my start date, or if there's any additional information I need to know.

Thank you again for this opportunity, and I look forward to working with you and the team.

Best regards,

[Your Name]

Email Sample 3: Accepting an Invitation for an Informational Interview

Subject: RE: Invitation to Informational Interview at DEF Company

Dear [Contact's Name],

Thank you for considering me for the opportunity to have an informational interview with you about your experience at DEF

Company. I'm excited to accept your invitation and learn more about your career path and the company.

Please let me know if there's anything I should prepare for the interview or if there are any specific topics you'd like to discuss. I'm available for any further questions or clarification before the interview.

Thank you again for your time, and I look forward to meeting you soon.

Best regards,
[Your Name]

Declining Invites Politely

Email Sample 1: Declining a Job Offer

Subject: Declining Job Offer for [Job Title]

Dear [Hiring Manager's Name],

Thank you for offering me the position of [Job Title] at ABC Company. I appreciate the time and effort you and the team have put into considering my application.

After careful consideration, I have decided to decline your job offer. Although I was impressed with the company and the position, I have decided to pursue other opportunities that are more aligned with my long-term career goals.

I value the professional relationship we have built throughout the hiring process, and I hope we can keep in touch. Please don't hesitate to reach out to me if there's anything I can assist you with in the future.

Thank you again for the opportunity, and I wish you and the company continued success.

Best regards,
[Your Name].

Email Sample 2: Declining an Invitation for an Event

Subject: Regretful Decline of Invitation to Attend [Event]

Dear [Event Organizer's Name],

Thank you for the invitation to attend [Event Name] on [Date] at [Location]. I appreciate the time and effort you have put into organizing the event and considering me as a participant.

Unfortunately, I regret to inform you that I will not be able to attend the event due to [Reason]. I understand the importance of this event and apologize for any inconvenience my absence may cause.

I wish you all the best for a successful event, and please keep me informed about any future events or opportunities to collaborate.

Thank you again for considering me, and I hope to have the opportunity to attend in the future.

Best regards,
[Your Name]

Email Sample 3: Declining an Invitation for a Meeting

Subject: Regretful Decline of Invitation to Meet

Dear [Inviter's Name],

Thank you for inviting me to meet with you on [Date] at [Location]. I appreciate the time and effort you have put into considering me as a participant.

Unfortunately, I regret to inform you that I will not be able to attend the meeting due to [Reason]. I understand the importance of the meeting and apologize for any inconvenience my absence may cause.

Please let me know if there's any way I can provide any assistance before or after the meeting. I value our professional relationship and hope to have the opportunity to collaborate in the future.

Thank you again for considering me, and I wish you all the best for a successful meeting.

Best regards,

[Your Name

Sending Job Applications

Email Sample 1: Cold Application

Subject: Job Application - Marketing Specialist Position

Dear [Hiring Manager's Name],

I hope this email finds you well. I am writing to express my interest in the Marketing Specialist position at [Company Name], as advertised on [Job Board/Company Website]. With my passion for marketing and

my strong analytical and creative skills, I believe I would be a valuable addition to your team.

I have a proven track record in developing and executing successful marketing strategies, leveraging both traditional and digital channels. In my previous role at XYZ Company, I was responsible for overseeing social media campaigns that resulted in a 30% increase in brand awareness within six months. Additionally, I led a cross-functional team in launching a new product, driving a 15% boost in sales within the first quarter.

I am impressed by [Company Name]'s innovative approach to marketing and your commitment to delivering exceptional results. Your recent campaign for [Project/Initiative] caught my attention, and I would love the opportunity to contribute my skills and insights to further your success.

Please find attached my resume for your review. I would greatly appreciate the chance to discuss my qualifications and how I can contribute to [Company Name] in more detail. I am available for a phone call or an in-person meeting at your convenience.

Thank you for considering my application. I look forward to hearing from you soon.

Sincerely,
[Your Name]
[Your Contact Information]

Email Sample 2: Referral Application

Subject: Referred Application - Experienced Software Engineer

Dear [Hiring Manager's Name],

I hope this email finds you well. I recently spoke with [Referrer's Name], who is a [Mutual Contact/Colleague] of ours, and they mentioned that [Company Name] is seeking an experienced Software Engineer. As an experienced professional in the field with a strong track record of delivering innovative solutions, I am excited to express my interest in joining your team.

With [X years] of experience in software development, I have successfully led the design and implementation of complex projects in both agile and waterfall environments. I am proficient in [relevant programming languages/technologies], and my expertise includes

[specific achievements or projects]. At my current position with [Current Company], I spearheaded the development of a new software module that increased system efficiency by 25%.

I am drawn to [Company Name]'s reputation for groundbreaking technologies and its commitment to pushing the boundaries of innovation. The recent advancements in [Technology/Project] showcased on your website further fueled my enthusiasm to contribute to your team's success.

Please find attached my resume for your consideration. I would be delighted to discuss how my skills and experiences align with the needs of [Company Name]. I am available for a phone call or an in-person interview at your convenience.

Thank you for your time and consideration. I look forward to the opportunity to contribute to the continued success of [Company Name].

Best regards,
[Your Name]
[Your Contact Information]

Email Sample 3: Follow-Up Application

Subject: Follow-up on Job Application - Sales Associate Position

Dear [Hiring Manager's Name],

I hope this email finds you well. I recently applied for the Sales Associate position at [Company Name] and wanted to follow up on my application. I am extremely excited about the opportunity to join your team and contribute to the continued growth and success of your organization.

After submitting my application, I have taken the time to further research [Company Name]'s market presence, customer base, and recent achievements. I am particularly impressed with your innovative sales strategies and the excellent customer satisfaction ratings you have consistently achieved.

With [X years] of experience in sales and a proven track record of exceeding targets, I am confident in my ability to drive revenue growth and deliver exceptional customer service. In my previous role at [Previous Company], I consistently surpassed my sales quotas by an average of 20% and received recognition for my outstanding performance.

I understand that you are likely receiving numerous applications, and I genuinely appreciate your time and consideration. If there are any additional materials or information, I can provide to support my application, please let me know.

Thank you once again for considering my application. I am eager to discuss my qualifications further and demonstrate my commitment to making a significant impact as a Sales Associate at [Company Name]. I am available for an interview at your convenience.

Best regards,
[Your Name]
[Your Contact Information]

CHAPTER 3 -

EMAIL

WRITING FOR

WORK AND

CAREER

Your 10 Markers

Ismail, my friend and colleague, was not your typical copywriter, but he had an uncanny ability to tweak ad copies that could turn heads and generate results. His passion and expertise lay in the world of online career consultancy, where he had founded and successfully ran his own firm.

When it comes to ad management, Ismail had a unique approach. Whenever he conducted outreach for his consultancy through ads, he wouldn't settle for just one creative. No, Ismail would craft about five different ad creatives, each presenting a unique angle. Even if none of them immediately hit the mark, he wouldn't be discouraged. Instead, he'd go back to the drawing board and create another set of five creatives with a completely different perspective.

Ismail's determination was truly remarkable. There were instances when his success in driving traffic and visitors to his website raised skepticism among ad networks. Some were quick to question the quality of his traffic, leading to suspensions or even bans. However, Ismail never let these setbacks deter him. While ad revenue was a secondary concern for him, he understood the importance of proving his case.

In the face of network suspensions, Ismail would tirelessly work to demonstrate the legitimacy and value of his traffic. His resilience was unmatched. Most times, he managed to get reinstated, not by simply accepting defeat, but by methodically proving the legitimacy of his efforts.

What stood out the most about Ismail was his refusal to take "no" for an answer. He was a living testament to the idea that success often requires a blend of creativity, determination, and resilience. Ismail's ability to pivot, adapt, and continuously improve his approach taught me valuable lessons about facing challenges head-on and never giving up easily.

In our fast-paced and competitive professional landscape, Ismail's story served as a constant reminder that setbacks are inevitable, but true success lies in the ability to overcome them with an unwavering spirit. I was fortunate to have Ismail as a friend and colleague, learning not only the art of effective ad copy but also the importance of persistence in the face of adversity.

Think of business writing as your secret weapon, the vibrant brushstrokes on the canvas of your career. It's the magical potion that can captivate your audience, inspire action, and leave a lasting impression. With every keystroke, you have the power to influence, persuade, and showcase your brilliance to the world.

But mastering the art of business writing is more than just stringing words together. It's about crafting messages that resonate, engage, and elicit a response. It's about finding the perfect balance between

professionalism and personality, creating a distinct voice that sets you apart in the crowded inbox.

We'll explore the art of concise yet compelling communication, ensuring your message gets straight to the point while captivating your recipients from the first sentence.

Get ready to delve into the universe of email writing etiquette – the unwritten rules that govern digital communication. We'll chart the tricky waters of tone, ensuring your words convey the right message and leave no room for misinterpretation. From formal to friendly, you will master the art of adapting to various situations and audiences.

When writing emails for work and career, there are several key considerations that can help you make a positive impact and achieve your desired outcomes. Here are 10 important things to keep in mind:

1. Purpose and Clarity: Clearly define the purpose of your email and ensure your message is concise, focused, and easy to understand. Avoid unnecessary details or ambiguity.

2. Professional Tone: Maintain a professional and respectful tone throughout your email. Use proper grammar, avoid slang or jargon, and be mindful of your language and phrasing.

3. Subject Line: Craft a compelling subject line that accurately reflects the content of your email and entices recipients to open it. Keep it concise and specific to grab attention.

4. Audience and Personalization: Consider the preferences, needs, and expectations of your recipients. Address them by name and tailor your message to their specific context whenever possible.

5. Email Structure: Use clear paragraphs, bullet points, or numbered lists to organize your thoughts and make your email easy to skim. Highlight important information and maintain logical flow.

6. Conciseness: Respect the time and attention of your recipients by keeping your email concise. Get to the point quickly and avoid unnecessary or redundant information.

7. Proofreading and Editing: Take the time to proofread your email for spelling, grammar, and punctuation errors. Ensure your

message is polished and error-free before hitting the send button.

8. Professional Sign-off: End your email with a professional closing, such as "Best regards" or "Sincerely," followed by your name and appropriate contact information (e.g., phone number, email signature).

9. Respectful and Timely Responses: Be prompt in responding to emails and show respect for others' time. Even if you don't have an immediate answer, acknowledge receipt and provide a timeframe for a more detailed response if needed.

10. Privacy and Confidentiality: Be mindful of privacy and confidentiality when sharing sensitive information. Use proper security measures and double-check recipients' email addresses to avoid accidental disclosure.

Remember, effective email communication can leave a lasting impression and contribute to your professional success. By following these guidelines, you'll enhance your ability to connect, engage, and achieve your goals in the workplace and beyond

For Salary Decrease and Increase

As a business owner, I've learned from my experiences that open communication with staff regarding salary adjustments is crucial for several reasons. Taking action without communication can lead to misunderstandings, erode trust, and negatively impact employee morale. Here's why I firmly believe in transparently communicating salary changes with my team:

Building Trust and Respect: Employees are the backbone of any successful business. When I communicate openly about salary adjustments, it shows that I value and respect their hard work and contributions. This trust-building process is vital for fostering a positive work environment and maintaining a strong employer-employee relationship.

Clarifying Expectations: Salary changes can be emotionally charged and create anxiety among employees. By discussing the reasons behind the adjustments and providing clear explanations, I can ensure that staff understands the factors considered in the decision-making process. This clarity helps manage expectations and reduces uncertainty.

Motivating and Recognizing Efforts: When staff members see that their dedication and achievements are acknowledged through salary adjustments, it serves as a powerful motivator. Recognition of their hard work reinforces a culture of appreciation and encourages employees to continue striving for excellence.

Addressing Concerns and Providing Support: Transparent communication opens the door for employees to express their concerns and seek support if needed. Some team members might need help adjusting their financial plans, while others might appreciate guidance on professional development to enhance their skills and career prospects.

Fostering a Positive Work Culture: A culture of open communication is essential for fostering a positive work environment. Employees are more likely to feel valued and engaged when they are kept informed about significant changes within the organization. This positive work culture contributes to higher job satisfaction and staff retention.

Navigating Difficult Times Together: During challenging economic periods, salary adjustments may be necessary to ensure the stability and longevity of the business. By communicating openly, I can help my team understand the broader context and the measures being taken to traverse through tough times together.

Demonstrating Integrity and Fairness: Transparent communication about salary changes demonstrates integrity and fairness in the decision-making process. When employees see that adjustments are made with clear and justifiable reasons, it builds their confidence in the organization's leadership.

Enhancing Company Reputation: A business with a reputation for open and honest communication is more likely to attract top talent. Prospective employees seek companies that value transparency and treat their staff with respect and fairness.

Empowering Employee Voice: Open communication empowers employees to voice their opinions and provide feedback. I value the input of my team members and believe that their perspectives are invaluable in shaping the organization's future.

Strengthening the Team Bond: When I communicate with my team about salary changes, it reinforces that we are a united and supportive team. We face challenges together and celebrate successes together, fostering a strong sense of camaraderie.

In conclusion, transparent communication with staff regarding salary adjustments is not just an ethical responsibility but a strategic move to maintain a motivated, engaged, and loyal workforce. By involving my team in the decision-making process and providing them with the necessary information, I can build a stronger and more resilient organization that thrives on trust and mutual respect.

For Salary Decrease:

Sample Email 1:
Subject: Understanding the Necessity of a Salary Adjustment

Dear Team,

I hope this email finds you all in good health and spirits. I am writing to address a matter of great importance, one that weighs heavily on all of us as we unravel these challenging times together.

As you are aware, the global economic landscape has been volatile, and our company has not been immune to its impact. We have explored various avenues to sustain our operations and support our valued employees during these uncertain times. Regrettably, one measure we must take to ensure the long-term stability of our organization is a temporary salary decrease across the company.

I want to assure you that this decision was not made lightly and was carefully considered. Our commitment to our team remains unwavering, and we are taking this step to protect jobs and maintain the strength of our company.

We understand the concerns and anxieties this announcement may evoke, and I want to emphasize that we are in this together. Our primary focus is to emerge from this period of uncertainty stronger and more resilient. We are actively exploring additional support initiatives and closely monitoring market conditions to restore salaries as soon as possible.

I sincerely appreciate your dedication and hard work during these trying times. Our team's unity and understanding will undoubtedly carry us through these challenges, and I am confident that together, we will overcome this obstacle.

If you have any questions or concerns, please do not hesitate to reach out to your department head or our HR team. We are committed to providing support and clarity during this period of adjustment.

Thank you for your continued commitment to our company. We will keep you informed of any updates, and your feedback is always welcome.

Sincerely,

[Your Name]
[Your Title]
[Company Name]

Sample Email 2:

Subject: *An Open Discussion on Salary Adjustments*

Dear Team,

I hope this email finds you all in good health and spirits. I write to you today with transparency and utmost respect for each and every member of our valued team.

As you know, the economic landscape has presented numerous challenges, and our company has not been immune to its effects. In light of the current situation, we are faced with the difficult task of implementing a temporary salary decrease for all employees.

We recognize that this news may be concerning and impact each individual differently. Our intention is to maintain the strength of our

organization, secure jobs, and foster a sustainable future for all of us. We believe that by sharing this burden collectively, we can overcome these trying times and emerge stronger together.

We are committed to open communication and hearing your thoughts and concerns. We understand that salary is an essential aspect of your livelihood, and we assure you that we are actively exploring avenues to restore salaries as soon as conditions permit.

Our commitment to you remains unwavering, and we are dedicated to providing resources and support during this transitional period. Should you have any questions or need assistance, please reach out to our HR department.

Thank you for your continued dedication and understanding. We are grateful for the resilience you have shown during these challenging times, and together, we will forge ahead with a shared vision of a brighter future.

Sincerely,

[Your Name]
[Your Title]

[Company Name]

Sample Email 3:

Subject: Empathy and Collaboration in Uncertain Times

Dear Team,

I hope you and your families are safe and well. In light of the current economic challenges, I am writing this email with a heavy heart but also with an unwavering commitment to each and every one of you.

As you may be aware, the business landscape has been severely impacted, requiring us to reevaluate our operations. We have made the difficult decision to implement a temporary salary decrease for all employees.

Please know that this decision was not taken lightly, and it was made only after exploring various options to sustain our business and preserve jobs. We understand the financial impact this may have on you and your loved ones, and we deeply empathize with the concerns this decision may raise.

Our priority is to stand together during these trying times, fostering an environment of empathy and collaboration. We are committed to maintaining open lines of communication and addressing any questions or concerns you may have.

Rest assured, we are actively monitoring the situation and are prepared to adapt as conditions change. Our shared goal is to emerge stronger and united from this period of uncertainty.

In the spirit of transparency, we will continue to keep you updated on any developments and progress. Our HR team is available to assist you, and we encourage you to reach out if you need support or guidance.

Thank you for your dedication, resilience, and understanding. Together, we will weather this storm and pave the way for a brighter tomorrow.

Sincerely,

[Your Name]
[Your Title]
[Company Name]

For Salary Increase:

Sample Email 1:
Subject: Celebrating Your Outstanding Contributions!

Dear [Team],

I hope this email finds you all in high spirits! I am thrilled to share some exciting news that brings a smile to my face and a sense of pride in our team.

Your dedication, hard work, and commitment to excellence have not gone unnoticed. As a result of your exceptional efforts and remarkable achievements, I am delighted to announce a well-deserved salary increase for each and every one of you!

This salary increase reflects our deep appreciation for your contributions and the vital role you play in driving our company's success. Your passion, creativity, and teamwork have propelled us to new heights, and we are excited to celebrate this milestone together.

The salary increase will be effective starting [date], and you will see the adjustments in your upcoming paychecks. Your HR team will be available to answer any questions you may have regarding this exciting development.

Once again, thank you for your unwavering commitment and dedication to our shared vision. This achievement is a testament to our thriving team spirit, and I look forward to our continued growth and success together.

Let's celebrate this momentous occasion and toast to a bright and prosperous future ahead!

Cheers,

[Your Name]
[Your Title]
[Company Name]

Sample Email 2:
Subject: Recognizing Your Stellar Performance with a Salary Boost!

Dear [Team],

I hope this email finds you in high spirits and excited for the journey ahead! Today, I am delighted to share some fantastic news that reflects the brilliance of our talented team.

Your outstanding performance, unwavering passion, and dedication to our company's mission have not gone unnoticed. We are incredibly proud of the tremendous impact you have made, and I am thrilled to announce that a well-deserved salary increase is on its way to you!

This salary boost is a testament to your continuous efforts and your relentless pursuit of excellence. Your contributions have been instrumental in driving our success, and we are grateful to have such an exceptional team by our side.

Starting [date], your increased salary will be reflected in your paycheck, acknowledging the value you bring to our organization. We understand that you may have questions, and our HR team is available to provide all the necessary support and guidance.

Your dedication has been the driving force behind our achievements, and we couldn't be prouder of the team we have built together. As we move forward, let's continue to aim high, dream big, and achieve even greater milestones!

Once again, congratulations on this well-deserved recognition. Together, we will continue to create a future filled with success, growth, and prosperity.

Thank you for being the heart and soul of our company.

Best regards,

[Your Name]
[Your Title]
[Company Name]

Sample Email 3:
Subject: Celebrating Your Success with a Salary Increase!

Dear [Team],

I hope this email finds you all feeling proud and energized! I am thrilled to share some fantastic news that is sure to make your day even brighter.

Your hard work, dedication, and relentless pursuit of excellence have paid off tremendously. As a result of your unwavering commitment to our company's goals and your exceptional performance, we are excited to announce a well-deserved salary increase for each one of you!

This salary increase is a testament to your success and the value you bring to our organization. Your talent and dedication have set the bar high for all of us, and we are thrilled to reward your efforts with this exciting recognition.

Starting [date], your salary increase will be implemented, and you will see the adjustments in your upcoming paychecks. Our HR team is here to answer any questions you may have and ensure a seamless transition.

Thank you for being the driving force behind our achievements and for constantly raising the bar. Your hard work and enthusiasm inspire us all, and we are incredibly proud to have you on our team.

Let's celebrate this well-earned success and look forward to even greater accomplishments together!

With gratitude,

[Your Name]
[Your Title]
[Company Name]

For Layoffs

I cannot emphasize enough the significance of transparent and empathetic communication with staff during times of layoffs. Not only does it help avoid potential litigation and associated issues, but it also preserves the integrity of our company and strengthens our bond with our employees. Allow me to share a few creative scenarios to illustrate why effective communication is vital:

Scenario 1: The Surprising Announcement

Imagine a scenario where employees arrive at work one morning to find out that some of their colleagues have been laid off without any prior communication. Word spreads quickly, and frustration, confusion, and fear start to ripple through the workplace. Employees begin to speculate about the reasons behind the layoffs, leading to resentment towards the management. This lack of communication not only damages staff morale but also opens the door to potential legal challenges as employees feel unfairly treated.

Scenario 2: The Ambiguous Memo

In another scenario, the management sends out a vague memo stating that there will be a reduction in workforce due to restructuring. However, no specific details or reasons are provided, leaving employees in the dark about the decision-making process. The lack of clarity leads to rumors and misunderstandings, heightening anxiety and stress among the remaining staff. As a result, the laid-off employees may seek legal counsel to explore their options, suspecting potential discrimination or wrongful termination.

Scenario 3: The Honest and Empathetic Approach

Now, envision a different scenario where the management takes an honest and empathetic approach. Prior to the layoff, they communicate

with employees about the challenging economic situation the company is facing, and they explain the necessity of streamlining operations. They hold open forums where employees can voice their concerns and ask questions, providing as much information as possible without compromising privacy.

By taking this approach, the management shows genuine care for their employees' well-being and ensures that they feel valued despite the difficult situation. They provide support resources, such as career counseling or job placement assistance, to help the affected employees transition to new opportunities. The remaining staff appreciates the transparent communication and the efforts made to treat the affected employees with dignity.

In this scenario, potential litigation and associated issues are significantly minimized. Employees feel respected and understand the reasons behind the layoffs, reducing the likelihood of legal challenges. The company is seen as compassionate and fair, and the remaining staff remains engaged and motivated to support the organization during the transition.

In conclusion, creative scenarios illustrate the critical role of effective communication during times of layoffs. By being transparent,

empathetic, and providing support, we can avoid potential legal battles, protect our company's reputation, and maintain a positive and cohesive work environment. Treating our employees with respect and dignity, even during challenging times, will undoubtedly lead to long-term benefits for both the company and its valued workforce.

Sample Email 1:

Subject: Addressing Difficult Decisions and Moving Forward Together

Dear Team,

I hope this email finds you well. I am writing to address a matter that is deeply difficult and weighs heavily on my heart. Due to unforeseen economic challenges, we are faced with the necessity of implementing a mass layoff within our organization.

This decision was not taken lightly, and it has been the result of extensive evaluation and contemplation. I want to emphasize that this layoff is not a reflection of your individual contributions or dedication. Instead, it is a measure we must take to ensure the long-term viability of our company.

As we steer through these trying times, please know that our commitment to supporting you remains unwavering. Our HR team will be providing comprehensive resources to assist you during this transitional period, including guidance on job placement, resume building, and access to career counseling.

Your contributions to our organization have been invaluable, and your time with us has made a significant impact. While this is an incredibly challenging moment, I am confident that you possess the resilience and talent to embark on new opportunities and succeed.

We will be conducting individual meetings to discuss the details of your transition, and you will be provided with the necessary information and assistance every step of the way.

Please know that you are not alone in this journey. We are a family, and your well-being remains our utmost priority. I deeply appreciate your dedication and the value you have brought to our team, and I am hopeful that our paths may cross again in the future.

Thank you for being a part of our organization's story. I wish you all the best as you embrace new beginnings and embark on your next adventure.

Sincerely,

[Your Name]
[Your Title]
[Company Name]

Sample Email 2:

Subject: A Message of Hope and Resilience During Challenging Times

Dear Team,

I hope this email finds you in good health and spirits. I am writing to share some difficult news, as we steer through an unprecedented period of uncertainty.

The current economic landscape has posed significant challenges for our company, and after careful consideration, we have made the difficult decision to initiate a mass layoff. This decision is deeply regrettable, and we recognize the impact it has on each and every one of you.

Please understand that this is not a reflection of your dedication, skills, or contributions. The decision has been made in response to external factors that have affected our industry and company performance.

During this challenging period, we are committed to providing support and resources to ease your transition. Our HR team will be available to assist with resume building, job search guidance, and any other support you may need as you explore new opportunities.

I want to express my heartfelt gratitude for your hard work and commitment during your time with us. Your contributions have been valuable, and I sincerely hope that your future holds success and fulfillment.

Remember that you are part of a strong and resilient team, and this layoff does not define your worth or capabilities. As you embark on new journeys, know that you carry with you the experience and skills gained here, which will undoubtedly lead to future achievements.

Please feel free to reach out to our HR team or myself with any questions or concerns you may have. We stand united in facing these challenges and are here to support you.

Thank you for being part of our team's journey. We wish you all the best in your future endeavors.

Warm regards,

[Your Name]
[Your Title]
[Company Name]

Sample Email 3:
Subject: Gratitude and Support During Times of Change

Dear Team,

I hope this message finds you well. Today, I must share some difficult news that affects us all. Due to the ongoing economic challenges, we have made the heart-wrenching decision to implement a mass layoff within our organization.

I want to be transparent and express that this decision is not taken lightly. It comes after extensive evaluation and with the deepest

consideration for each team member. Our company is facing unprecedented times, and we must take measures to ensure its long-term sustainability.

During this period of transition, our priority is to provide unwavering support to you. Our HR team has prepared comprehensive resources, including career counseling, job placement assistance, and severance packages to aid you in your next steps.

I want to extend my heartfelt gratitude for the dedication and passion you have brought to our organization. Your contributions have played a vital role in our success, and your presence will be deeply missed.

I understand that this is an unsettling time, and I encourage you to lean on the support of your colleagues and our HR team as you explore new opportunities. Together, we will journey through these changes and emerge stronger on the other side.

The memory of our collective achievements will remain in our hearts, and the relationships forged will continue to hold value beyond this chapter.

Please know that you have our unwavering support, and we are here to answer any questions or provide assistance throughout this transition.

With sincere gratitude and best wishes,

[Your Name]
[Your Title]
[Company Name]

The Petty Version
Sample Email 1:
Subject: Termination of Employment

Dear [Staff Member],

I hope this email finds you well. I am writing to inform you that, after careful consideration and review of your recent actions and conduct, we have made the difficult decision to terminate your employment with [Company Name], effective immediately.

We have consistently communicated our expectations regarding professional behavior and conduct in the workplace. Unfortunately, your actions have not aligned with these expectations, and they have had a detrimental impact on the team and our company's reputation.

I want to acknowledge your past contributions to our organization; however, the recent incidents have left us with no alternative but to take this step. We value integrity, accountability, and respect among our team members, and we cannot compromise on these core principles.

Please arrange to collect your personal belongings from your workspace, and our HR team will assist you with the necessary paperwork and the final settlement of your dues.

We wish you success in your future endeavors, and we hope that you will take this opportunity for self-reflection and growth.

Sincerely,

[Your Name]
[Your Title]
[Company Name]

Sample Email 2:

Subject: Termination of Employment

Dear [Staff Member],

I hope this email finds you well. I regret to inform you that your employment with [Company Name] is being terminated, effective [date].

Over the past [duration], we have documented several incidents of poor performance and frequent violations of company policies. Despite previous counseling and support to improve your performance, we have not seen the desired progress.

Our commitment to maintaining a productive and harmonious work environment compels us to take this decision. It is essential for our team's success that each member meets the performance standards set by the company.

Please schedule a meeting with our HR team to complete the necessary formalities related to your departure.

Thank you for your service to our organization, and we wish you the best in your future endeavors.

Sincerely,

[Your Name]
[Your Title]
[Company Name]

Sample Email 3:
Subject: Termination of Employment

Dear [Staff Member],

I hope this message finds you well. I am writing to inform you that, regrettably, we are terminating your employment with [Company Name], effective [date].

Your recent actions have shown a pattern of behavior that is incompatible with our company's values and code of conduct. We pride ourselves on maintaining a positive and inclusive work environment, and your behavior has compromised this principle.

Our team deserves to work in an environment where mutual respect and professionalism are upheld. It is with a heavy heart that we must part ways, but we believe it is in the best interest of the team and the organization as a whole.

Please coordinate with our HR department to complete the necessary formalities and obtain your final paycheck.

We wish you success in your future endeavors and hope that this experience serves as an opportunity for personal growth and development.

Sincerely,

[Your Name]
[Your Title]
[Company Name]

How to Detect Passive Aggressive Tones in Emails

One of my first ever jobs was as a tutor teaching commerce in a secondary school. I found myself dealing with various challenges and joys in my day-to-day work. One particular challenge I encountered was deciphering the true intentions behind the emails I received from one of the head teachers. While the emails appeared professional on the surface, I couldn't shake the feeling that there was an underlying

passive-aggressive tone in many of them. Learning to detect these tones and resolving the issue became a valuable skill that not only improved my communication with the head teacher but also strengthened our working relationship.

Detecting passive-aggressive tones in emails can be tricky, but there are certain red flags to look out for. Initially, I noticed that the head teacher's messages often began with seemingly polite openings, but the content would quickly veer into vague complaints or criticism. For instance, in one email, she praised my dedication to the students but then subtly mentioned that my lesson plans needed "further improvements." This was a classic passive-aggressive tactic—appearing positive on the surface while delivering negative feedback.

Another key indicator was the excessive use of smiley faces or exclamation marks in inappropriate places. In one instance, the head teacher mentioned that she "loved" my recent teaching approach, but the overabundance of exclamation marks seemed insincere. It felt like she was using them to sugarcoat her true feelings, creating an atmosphere of faux enthusiasm.

Furthermore, passive-aggressive emails often included subtle guilt trips or attempts to make me question my own abilities. For example, when I couldn't attend a staff meeting due to prior commitments, she replied with an email saying, "Oh, no worries at all! We just missed an excellent opportunity to discuss some vital updates, but I'm sure you had other priorities." This made me feel guilty for prioritizing other commitments and seemed like an attempt to undermine my choices.

Recognizing these patterns in her emails was crucial, but it was equally important not to jump to conclusions. I took a step back and re-read her messages before responding emotionally. This allowed me to separate my initial emotional reaction from the actual content and identify any passive-aggressive undertones.

To resolve this issue, I decided to address the situation directly but tactfully. I scheduled a one-on-one meeting with the head teacher, expressing my appreciation for her guidance and support while also mentioning that I had noticed some unclear elements in her emails that I wanted to better understand. I gave specific examples without being confrontational and asked for clarification on her expectations. This approach allowed me to avoid a confrontational tone and instead fostered open communication.

To my surprise, the head teacher seemed receptive to my concerns. She admitted that she hadn't been aware of her passive-aggressive

tendencies and appreciated my honest feedback. She explained that she often felt overwhelmed with her workload and acknowledged that her communication style needed improvement. From then on, she made a conscious effort to be more direct and constructive in her emails.

As time passed, our communication improved significantly. The head teacher's emails became more concise and specific, allowing me to better understand her expectations and address any concerns promptly. This positive change not only eased my work as a tutor but also contributed to a healthier and more collaborative school environment.

In conclusion, detecting passive-aggressive tones in emails requires careful observation and a non-judgmental approach. Addressing the issue directly and with empathy can lead to positive outcomes and strengthen professional relationships. My experience as a tutor taught me the importance of effective communication and the impact it can have on fostering a supportive and productive work environment.

Detecting passive-aggressive tones in emails can be quite challenging, but here are some tips that may help:

- Read the email thoroughly: Take your time to carefully read and understand the content of the email. Pay attention to any

underlying tones or subtle hints that may indicate passive-aggressive behavior.

- Look for indirect language: Passive-aggressive individuals often use vague or ambiguous language to mask their true feelings. Elements like sarcasm, excessive use of exclamation marks, or over-politeness can be signs of passive aggression.

- Note contradictory statements: Passive-aggressive emails may contain contradictory statements. They might express agreement or support, but their overall tone may suggest something entirely different. Look for hidden meanings behind such contradictions.

- Identify veiled insults or critique: Passive-aggressive emails frequently include veiled insults, criticism, or blame. They might praise your work superficially while subtly pointing out areas of improvement or making negative comments.

- Pay attention to excessive use of "just" or "fine": Passive aggression can be reflected in the use of words like "just" or "fine." For example, saying "It's just a suggestion" might indicate disapproval rather than a genuine suggestion.

- Consider the context: Understanding the context of the email can help in detecting passive aggression. If you have been experiencing conflicts or tension with the sender, it's more likely that their email contains a passive-aggressive tone.

- Trust your instincts: Sometimes, you may have a gut feeling that an email is passive-aggressive, even if the language seems polite. Trust your instincts and look for other subtle clues that support your impression.

Remember, it's important to communicate openly and address any potential issues directly. If you find a passive-aggressive tone in an email, you can seek clarification or address the issue with the sender in a calm and assertive

CHAPTER 4 –

EMAIL

WRITING FOR

BUILDING A

BUSINESS

Effective Copywriting and Storytelling

As an e-commerce entrepreneur selling digital products (started with household and lifestyle products as a student) through Facebook ads and funnels, I have learned firsthand the immense power of effective copywriting and storytelling in driving sales and building a loyal customer base. I will share my experiences and insights on how mastering the art of copywriting and storytelling has transformed my business and can do the same for yours.

The Magic of Words: Why Copywriting Matters

In the digital age, where attention spans are short and competition is fierce, words hold the key to capturing your audience's attention and igniting their interest. Copywriting is the art of using persuasive language to communicate your brand's message, evoke emotions, and ultimately compel your audience to take action. In the context of e-commerce, this action typically involves making a purchase or engaging with your brand in some meaningful way.

When I first started my e-commerce venture, I quickly realized that crafting compelling copy for my product descriptions, ad headlines, and landing pages was non-negotiable. An ordinary, lackluster description could lead potential customers to scroll past my ad, while a well-crafted one could stop them in their tracks and draw them into my funnel.

The Power of Storytelling: Connecting with Your Audience-
At the heart of effective copywriting lies storytelling—the art of weaving narratives that resonate with your audience on a deeper level. I discovered that by incorporating stories into my marketing efforts, I could establish a genuine connection with my potential customers.

For instance, instead of merely listing the features of a lifestyle product, I started creating stories around how these products enhanced

The Business Writing Guide

people's lives. I shared anecdotes of customers who had experienced positive transformations after using my products. These stories not only showcased the value of the products but also painted a vivid picture of the desired lifestyle my audience aspired to.

Identifying Your Target Audience: The Foundation of Effective Copy -

In the world of e-commerce, not all customers are created equal. Knowing your target audience inside out is crucial for crafting copy that truly resonates. I delved into market research, understanding the pain points, desires, and aspirations of my ideal customers. This knowledge became the foundation for my copywriting efforts.

By addressing my audience's specific needs and desires, my ads and funnels started generating better results. Whether it was a busy mom looking for time-saving solutions or a fitness enthusiast seeking high-quality gear, I tailored my copy to speak directly to them. The more targeted and personalized my messaging became, the more my audience responded positively.

The Art of Persuasion: Utilizing Psychological Triggers

Effective copywriting is rooted in psychology. By tapping into certain psychological triggers, I could influence my audience's decision-making process. Some of the key psychological triggers I incorporated into my copy included:

1. Fear of Missing Out (FOMO): Creating a sense of urgency through limited-time offers or limited stock availability drove customers to take immediate action.

2. Social Proof: Highlighting positive reviews and testimonials from satisfied customers reassured potential buyers that they were making a wise choice.

3. Emotional Appeals: Leveraging emotions like joy, nostalgia, or relief helped form stronger connections with my audience and compelled them to make purchases based on their feelings.

4. Scarcity: Emphasizing that certain products were available in limited quantities made them appear more desirable and exclusive.

Mastering the Funnel: Crafting a Seamless Customer Journey

Effective copywriting goes hand in hand with a well-structured sales funnel. The funnel guides potential customers through a series of steps, from awareness to conversion.

Each stage of the funnel requires unique copy and storytelling strategies.

1. Awareness Stage: Attracting attention through eye-catching ad headlines and compelling visuals is vital in this stage. I focused on piquing curiosity and generating interest.

2. Consideration Stage: As potential customers entered the consideration stage, I provided more in-depth information about my products, using persuasive copy to nurture their interest.

3. Conversion Stage: This is the critical stage where potential customers turn into paying customers. My copy at this stage emphasized the value and benefits of the products and included strong calls-to-action to prompt immediate purchases.

4. Post-Purchase Stage: After a successful sale, I continued to engage with my customers through personalized thank-you

messages and relevant content to encourage repeat purchases and foster brand loyalty.

5. Testing, Analyzing, and Iterating: The Continuous Journey: Copywriting in the any form is not a one-and-done endeavor. It requires constant testing, analyzing data, and iterating based on the results. I meticulously tracked the performance of my ads and funnels, analyzing which copies and storytelling tactics yielded the best results.

Through A/B testing, I experimented with different ad copies, headlines, and storytelling angles. Over time, I learned what resonated most with my audience, enabling me to refine my approach and optimize conversions.

The Human Touch: Building Authenticity and Trust

In the digital world, where automation and chatbots are prevalent, injecting a human touch into your copy can make a world of difference. I engaged in conversations with my customers, responding to their inquiries and feedback promptly. I also utilized email marketing to establish a more personal connection, sharing stories and updates that resonated with my audience.

Building authenticity and trust through genuine interactions was a cornerstone of my copywriting strategy. When customers felt valued and heard, they were more likely to become loyal brand advocates.

I have come to understand that copywriting and storytelling are not merely tools for selling products; they are bridges that connect my brand with my audience. Through crafting compelling narratives, tapping into psychological triggers, and building trust, I have seen my business grow and flourish.

Effective copywriting is an ever-evolving journey—one that requires understanding your target audience, harnessing the power of storytelling, and continually fine-tuning your approach. By embracing the magic of words and using them thoughtfully, you can create a powerful impact, driving sales and fostering lasting connections with your customers in the vast and dynamic world of e-commerce.

One of the most remarkable ad copywriting stories of this century comes from the "Dove Real Beauty" campaign, launched by Unilever's personal care brand, Dove, in 2004. The campaign aimed to challenge conventional beauty standards and celebrate the diversity and authenticity of women's bodies.

The pivotal moment in the campaign was the creation of the "Dove Evolution" commercial, released in 2006. The ad depicted the transformation of an average-looking woman into a glamorous model through the use of makeup, professional hairstyling, and extensive post-production editing. The powerful message behind the ad was that the unrealistic beauty ideals portrayed in the media were unattainable and that women should embrace their natural beauty instead.

The ad copy was minimal but impactful. It simply stated, "No wonder our perception of beauty is distorted," highlighting the negative influence of media manipulation on society's perception of beauty. The ad went viral, generating widespread discussion and sparking a global conversation about the impact of media imagery on self-esteem.

The "Dove Evolution" ad was not only a brilliant piece of storytelling but also a testament to the effectiveness of concise and thought-provoking ad copy. It challenged traditional advertising by presenting an honest narrative that resonated with people across different cultures and age groups.

The success of the "Dove Real Beauty" campaign continued with subsequent ads, such as the "Dove Sketches" campaign, which showcased women describing themselves to a forensic sketch artist.

The stark contrast between how women saw themselves and how others perceived them highlighted the need for self-acceptance and the importance of recognizing one's true beauty.

Overall, the "Dove Real Beauty" campaign's ad copywriting and storytelling approach had a profound impact on society, igniting conversations about body image, self-esteem, and redefining beauty standards. It serves as an exemplary case study for marketers and copywriters looking to create campaigns that resonate with audiences on a deeper level and inspire positive change.

Copywriting and storytelling are closely related and often overlap. Copywriting requires a clear and concise message, while storytelling is about creating a narrative that engages readers. Both need to use language that resonates with the audience, and both need to evoke emotion. Copywriting often uses storytelling techniques to create an emotional connection with the reader, while storytelling can incorporate facts and figures to help explain the story. In both cases, the goal is to create an engaging, memorable experience that leads to action.

Copywriting and storytelling are two of the most important skills to have in any career. The ability to tell your story clearly and effectively

is crucial for attracting clients, building trust with them, and making them feel like they're being heard. But what exactly does this mean?

A lot of copywriting and storytelling can be boiled down to a simple formula.

The formula is:

Start with a problem.

Show how you can solve it.

End with a call to action (CTA).

Use "you" to target the reader and make them comfortable

One of the most important things you can do to make your copy feel more personal is to use "you" instead of "I," "we," or any other form of possessive. This can be done in both written and spoken language, so don't worry about being too wordy when it comes to this one! Just make sure that each time you write about yourself, you add an extra touch of emotion by using this simple trick.

If someone else is speaking for you (and they should be!), then there's no need for them to use the word "your." Instead, just say something like: "I'm happy that we've been able to work together so far." Or: "It was great meeting up again at XYZ conference." Your colleagues will love your style because it makes them feel like an important part of something bigger than themselves—which means more loyalty from everyone involved!

You want to build an emotional connection with the reader.

There are several ways to create an emotional connection with the reader. The most important is by giving them a sense of belonging, and making them feel like you are talking directly to them. Humor can be a great tool for doing this, as well as personal stories from your life that tie into the topic at hand.

- Always offer readers a little bit of hope.
- Show how you can help them.
- Make it clear that you are on their side.
- Give them a reason to trust you
- Try to not let your own bias cloud your perspective.

When you write copy, it's important to keep in mind that your perspective may be a little biased. You want to make sure that what you write doesn't let those biases get in the way of telling a good story or writing compelling copy.

For example, if you're an engineer and someone asks you for help designing their product, the first thing they likely want is clear

directions on how to use it. But what if they ask for something more complex? What should they do then? Would you be able to give them clear instructions on how this tool could solve their problems without getting into technical details about why certain parts work better than others (or why there are no parts at all)? That might mean writing up some features from scratch instead of just listening as someone tells them about their needs and limitations until everyone agrees upon something concrete enough for implementation purposes."

Not everything has to be so serious all the time.

You don't have to be so serious all the time.

Humor is a great way to connect with your audience, but it's also an effective tool for standing out from the crowd. Humor can help you be more authentic, which is especially important in today's fast-paced world where people are constantly looking for new ways to communicate with each other and share their stories.

The key is to focus on building trust with the reader by presenting yourself as someone who understands their situation.

You can use the word "you" to make the reader feel like you are speaking directly to them. If you're writing a blog post or landing page, try this:

Use the word "you" in your headline, as well as throughout the copy. For example: "You don't want to waste money on unnecessary products."

Show empathy by showing that you understand their situation and how it might affect them personally (e.g., "I know how frustrating it is having an overstuffed closet").

Avoid being too serious or emotional; instead focus on making people laugh or smile when they read what you have written.

We've covered a lot of ground here, but really the takeaway is that good copywriting can be as simple as being yourself and offering readers a helping hand when they need it.

Learning Cold Emailing

When I founded my own copywriting and marketing agency, I embarked on an exciting journey of building my business from the ground up. One of the most challenging yet rewarding aspects of this journey was utilizing cold calling techniques, specifically cold emailing, to pitch CEOs and decision-makers about our content marketing services. This piece - input in browser https://fortifiedthinking.com/index.php/2023/11/06/how-to-build-a-perfect-sales-pitch-a-journey-of-trial-transformation-and-triumph/) details every step I took till I hit the sweet spot.

Through dedication, consistency, and a willingness to experiment, I was able to secure a game-changing contract via an interview for Blockleaders with Jordan, the CEO of Itembanc.

The Beginnings: Embracing Cold Emailing as a Strategy

When I started my agency, I knew that I needed to be proactive in reaching out to potential clients. Cold emailing seemed like an effective way to introduce my services to CEOs and decision-makers without the pressure of an immediate response. The idea of being able to showcase my agency's value through well-crafted emails was intriguing.

I began by researching and creating a list of companies whose values aligned with ours and whose content marketing strategies could benefit from our expertise. The list management process was crucial, as it ensured that I targeted the right audience with personalized and relevant messages.

Consistency Pays Off: The Power of Staying the Course

I quickly learned that cold emailing was not a one-shot strategy; it required consistency and patience. I set a daily goal to send out a specific number of cold emails, knowing that each one was an opportunity to make a connection and potentially land a client. Some

days were discouraging, with minimal responses or outright rejections, but I reminded myself that persistence was key.

Crafting Compelling Cold Emails: Standing Out in the Inbox

I focused on crafting compelling and personalized cold emails that would stand out in the recipients' crowded inboxes. Generic, spammy emails were not the way to go. Instead, I researched each company and its CEO, tailoring my message to address their specific pain points and goals.

The subject line was crucial—it needed to be attention-grabbing while not coming across as clickbait. I experimented with different subject lines to see which ones yielded better open rates. Over time, I found that subject lines that piqued curiosity or addressed a challenge the CEO might be facing worked best.

In the body of the email, I avoided lengthy pitches and focused on delivering value succinctly. I highlighted our agency's expertise, relevant success stories, and how we could help them achieve their content marketing goals. Ending with a clear call-to-action invited them to take the next step.

Embracing Rejection: Learning and Adapting

Rejection was inevitable, but I chose to view it as an opportunity for growth. I carefully analyzed the emails that received negative or no responses and sought to understand why they might not have resonated. Perhaps my messaging was too generic, or the timing wasn't right. By learning from these experiences, I adapted my approach and improved my emails over time.

The Breakthrough: Meeting Jordan of Itembanc

After weeks of consistent cold emailing, my breakthrough moment finally arrived. I received a response from Jordan, the CEO of Itembanc, expressing interest in a call to discuss our content marketing services. This was a turning point for my agency, and I was determined to make the most of it.

During our call, I demonstrated a genuine understanding of Itembanc's brand and challenges. I showcased our success stories and explained how our content marketing strategies could elevate their online presence and drive business growth. Our conversation was open, honest, and collaborative.

Sealing the Deal: Building a Lasting Partnership

My diligence and perseverance had paid off. Jordan was impressed with our approach and saw the potential value we could bring to his company. We negotiated terms, finalized the contract, and thus began a fruitful partnership with Itembanc.

My journey in building my copywriting and marketing agency using cold emailing techniques taught me the importance of consistency, persistence, and adaptability. Cold emailing is not an easy road, but it can be a powerful tool for reaching decision-makers and securing valuable contracts.

By refining my cold emailing strategy, experimenting with different approaches, and maintaining a genuine and personalized approach, I was able to connect with Jordan and make a lasting impact on his company's content marketing campaign. Cold emailing, when done right, is not just about landing a deal—it's about building meaningful relationships and delivering value to clients, ultimately shaping the success of my agency.

If you want to get the results from your cold email, then it is important that you write them correctly. This means keeping in mind what your audience is looking for and how they are likely to respond to your message. In this article we will go through all of the steps of writing a successful cold email so that when you send one out next time there will be no doubt about its effectiveness!

Graph 2.0 – Email Open Rate by How Long the Subject Line is

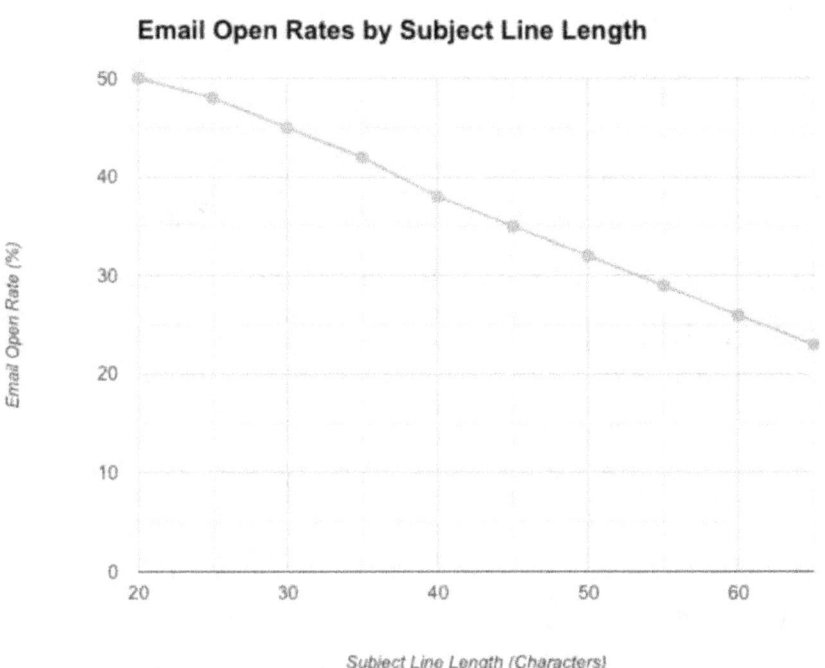

Before you start writing your cold email, do your research.

- Know your audience.
- Know what they want and need.
- Write a good email.

Open your cold email with a compliment.

When you open your cold email to a prospect, you want to start off with a compliment.

- Don't be too generic or lie about yourself or the company.
- Don't be too personal or forwardly flirty in your opening lines.

Get to the point.

To be clear, this is not the time to get into a long-winded email exchange. You don't need to waste time on small talk and beating around the bush. Make sure your reader knows what you're looking for in no uncertain terms:

- Get straight to business by saying "Hi! I'm interested in [insert job title]. If you could tell me more about how I can help [insert company name], that would be awesome."
- Don't make them guess what you're asking for either—be direct about it!

Explain what you want and why you want it.

Cold emails are not the best way to get your foot in the door. They're more of a "here's my resume" than an actual pitch for something specific. So, why do companies still use cold emails? Because it's

easy and fast! But if you want that job, then you need to make sure that your cold email gets results—and not just in the inboxes of whoever receives it.

It's important that you explain what you want and why you want it from them (and don't just say "I'm interested"). This will help show that they're hiring someone who has done their research on the company, has relevant experience for their position and is a good fit for both parties involved: both hiring managers or potential employees may benefit from reading this email if they're looking into making changes at work themselves!

In addition: give them contact details so they know where they can reach out if needed

Keep it short.

- Don't try to be funny or clever.
- Don't give too much detail, especially if the person you're emailing hasn't asked for it yet (like when they ask for a resume). They may not need all of the information in this cold email!

If you find yourself having trouble keeping your message focused on what they want, then there's a good chance that they'll just delete

your email instead of reading it and responding with interest. It's better if they just don't respond at all than waste their time reading something that doesn't help them get what they want out of life—which is usually more than just money!

Close with a call to action.

The last thing you want to do is confuse your recipient. You want them to be able to follow through on whatever it is that you're asking for, so make sure the call-to-action (CTA) is clear and concise.

A strong CTA can be:

- A deadline: "We'll pay $3,000 in 3 days."
- Specific actions: "Send us 15 articles on how we can help our readers."
- Something with a time frame like "within 24 hours," or even better than that: "by next Monday morning" because it gives you enough time but not too much!

Be prepared for rejection.

Expect to get rejected. This is part of the process, and if you don't expect it, then it's likely to surprise you. It shouldn't be a personal attack on you or your skills—it's just a reflection on the quality of your product or service. If someone rejects your email campaign, this

doesn't mean that they hate what you're offering; instead, it means that they don't think it will help them achieve their goals in any way at all (or maybe even worse: that they think something else would).

It pays to remember this when writing cold emails: rejection isn't about being mean; it's about being honest with yourself about whether or not what we're offering will work for our customer/client/whatever terminology fits best here

Cold emails can be effective but it is important to do them right.

Cold emails are a useful tool for getting results, but they can only be used if you know how to write them. Here are some tips on how to make sure that cold emails land with the right person:

- Research the person's name and email address before sending the message. If possible, try searching their name in Google or LinkedIn (if they have one). This will help you find information about them that might not be on their website or social profiles. You should also include links when possible so people can see what else about them interests you!
- Open with a compliment—it shows respect for them and makes it more likely that they will respond positively!
- Get straight into it by explaining why this is important for both parties involved; don't waste time talking about yourself first

unless absolutely necessary (so don't mention what kind of business opportunity it could lead toward).

- Explain exactly what exactly do want out of this exchange - don't leave things up in the air until later down the line when there's no way back anymore! For example: "I'm looking forward working closely together over emailing regularly."

Cold emailing can be a great way to get your message across, but it's not always easy. You need to know what you're doing and how to do it right.

SAMPLES

1. Cold Email for a Software Development Agency

Subject: Optimizing Your Software Solutions for Greater Efficiency

Dear [Recipient's Name],

I hope this email finds you well. My name is [Your Name], and I represent [Your Company Name], a leading software development agency specializing in creating innovative solutions for businesses like yours.

I noticed that [Recipient's Company] is making remarkable strides in [industry/niche], and I believe that we can contribute to your success by optimizing your software solutions for greater efficiency and seamless user experiences. Our team of skilled developers has a proven track record in creating customized applications that align perfectly with our clients' goals.

I'd love to arrange a brief call at your earliest convenience to discuss how our services can add value to [Recipient's Company] and assist you in achieving your objectives. Please let me know a suitable time, and I'll be more than happy to accommodate.

Thank you for considering us as a potential partner. I look forward to hearing from you soon.

Best regards,
[Your Name]
[Your Title]
[Your Company Name]
[Your Contact Information]

2. Cold Email for a Personal Fitness Trainer
Subject: Achieve Your Fitness Goals with Expert Guidance

Dear [Recipient's Name],

I hope this email finds you in good health. My name is [Your Name], and I'm a certified personal fitness trainer with a passion for helping individuals like you achieve their fitness goals.

I noticed that you're committed to living a healthy lifestyle, and I genuinely admire your dedication. As someone who's transformed the lives of many clients through personalized workout routines and nutritional guidance, I'm confident that I can assist you in reaching your fitness objectives.

Whether you're aiming to build strength, lose weight, or enhance overall well-being, my tailored programs are designed to suit your specific needs and fit seamlessly into your busy schedule.

If you're interested in discussing your fitness aspirations further, I'd love to arrange a complimentary consultation to learn more about your goals and share how my expertise can be of service to you.

Thank you for considering my offer. Let's work together to make your fitness journey a resounding success!

Sincerely,
[Your Name]
Certified Personal Fitness Trainer
[Your Contact Information]

3. Cold Email for a Content Marketing Agency

Subject: Elevate Your Brand's Storytelling and Engagement

Dear [Recipient's Name],

I hope this email finds you having a productive day. My name is [Your Name], and I'm reaching out on behalf of [Your Company Name], a leading content marketing agency dedicated to helping businesses like yours stand out in the digital landscape.

I've been following [Recipient's Company] for some time and have been impressed with your commitment to delivering top-notch

products and services. However, I noticed that your content storytelling and engagement could be further enhanced to resonate more deeply with your target audience.

At [Your Company Name], we specialize in crafting captivating content strategies that foster genuine connections with your customers, increase brand loyalty, and drive significant ROI.

I'd love to discuss how we can collaborate to elevate your brand's storytelling efforts and strengthen your online presence. Let me know when it's convenient for you, and I'll be more than happy to schedule a call.

Thank you for your time, and I look forward to the possibility of partnering with [Recipient's Company].

Warm regards,
[Your Name]
Content Marketing Specialist
[Your Company Name]
[Your Contact Information]

4. Cold Email for a Wedding Photography Business
Subject: Capturing Everlasting Memories of Your Special Day

Dear [Recipient's Name],

Congratulations on your upcoming wedding! My name is [Your Name], and I'm a passionate wedding photographer with a keen eye for capturing beautiful and authentic moments.

I recently came across your wedding announcement and couldn't help but feel inspired by the love and excitement that surrounds you and your partner. As a professional photographer, my goal is to preserve these cherished memories for you to relive for generations to come.

With an artistic approach and attention to detail, I specialize in candid and artistic photography that encapsulates the essence of your love story. I believe that every couple deserves to have a collection of images that truly reflect their unique journey.

If you're interested in discussing your photography needs further or would like to see some samples of my work, please don't hesitate to reach out. I would be honored to be a part of your special day.

Thank you for considering my services, and I eagerly await the opportunity to create lasting memories with you.

Best regards,
[Your Name]
Professional Wedding Photographer
[Your Contact Information]

5. Cold Email for a Home Cleaning Service

Subject: Enjoy a Spotless Home with Our Reliable Cleaning Services

Dear [Recipient's Name],

I hope this email finds you well. I'm [Your Name], and I represent [Your Company Name], a trusted and professional home cleaning service dedicated to making your life easier.

Keeping a tidy and clean home can be a demanding task, especially with today's busy schedules. That's where our team comes in to provide

you with the much-needed peace of mind and a spotless living environment.

At [Your Company Name], we pride ourselves on our attention to detail and personalized approach. Our experienced and reliable cleaners are committed to exceeding your expectations, ensuring your home is immaculate and ready for you to enjoy.

We'd love to discuss your cleaning requirements and tailor a cleaning plan that fits your schedule and preferences. Please feel free to contact us at your convenience, and we'll be happy to assist you.

Thank you for considering [Your Company Name] as your home cleaning partner. We look forward to the opportunity to serve you.

Kind regards,
[Your Name]
Home Cleaning Specialist
[Your Company Name]
[Your Contact Information]

Note: When sending cold emails, always ensure that you have obtained proper permission to reach out to the recipients,

especially in compliance with applicable data protection laws and regulations. Additionally, make sure to follow best practices for cold emailing to increase the chances of a positive response.

For Business Negotiations

In the fast-paced and competitive world of business negotiations, effective written communication plays a pivotal role in reaching successful agreements and building strong partnerships. Back and forth negotiations, where proposals and counteroffers are exchanged multiple times, require a unique set of business writing modalities to ensure clarity, professionalism, and strategic communication.

In this chapter, we will explore the essential elements of business writing in back and forth negotiations through real-life and fictional corporate world scenarios.

1. Establishing a Clear Purpose and Tone

Scenario: Imagine you are the sales director of a software company negotiating a partnership with a potential client for the implementation of a new CRM system. The negotiations have been ongoing for weeks, and both parties have exchanged several proposals and counteroffers.

Business Writing Modality: In back and forth negotiations, maintaining a clear and professional tone is vital. Ensure that your writing conveys a sense of collaboration and mutual interest in finding a win-win solution. Avoid language that might be perceived as aggressive or confrontational.

Example:

Dear [Recipient's Name],

I hope this email finds you well. As we continue our discussions on the CRM implementation project, I wanted to express our commitment to exploring the best possible solution for [Recipient's Company]. Our

goal is to establish a partnership that drives long-term growth and success for both our organizations.

We have carefully reviewed your latest proposal and appreciate the efforts you have put into tailoring it to our needs. To address some specific requirements from our end, we have made a few revisions to our initial offer. We believe these changes will strengthen our collaboration and deliver exceptional results.

Looking forward to your insights on our revised proposal and working together to finalize the details that align seamlessly with both our visions.

Best regards,
[Your Name]
Sales Director, [Your Company Name]

2. Focusing on Value Proposition and Benefits

Scenario: In another scenario, you are an entrepreneur negotiating with potential investors for funding to scale your sustainable packaging startup. The investors have expressed concerns about the market competition and expected returns.

Business Writing Modality: In back and forth negotiations, it's essential to emphasize the value proposition and the benefits of your proposal. Address the investors' concerns thoughtfully and offer data-driven evidence of your market research and growth potential.

Example:

Dear [Recipient's Name],

I appreciate your diligence in evaluating our business plan and potential investment in [Your Company Name]. I understand the importance of considering market competition and risk factors in the decision-making process.

As we pilot through the negotiation process, I would like to take this opportunity to emphasize the unique value proposition of our sustainable packaging solutions. Our market research indicates a growing consumer demand for eco-friendly alternatives, and our innovative products are designed to address the pressing environmental challenges while maintaining a competitive edge.

In the current landscape, consumers are actively seeking brands that demonstrate environmental responsibility. By partnering with [Your

Company Name], you have the opportunity to be at the forefront of this industry shift and capitalize on a rapidly expanding market.

I would be delighted to share additional data and case studies that illustrate the potential ROI of investing in our sustainable packaging venture.

Thank you for your consideration, and I look forward to further discussions.

Best regards,
[Your Name]
Founder, [Your Company Name]

3. Addressing Objections and Providing Solutions

Scenario: As a project manager, you are negotiating with a potential vendor for a crucial construction project. The vendor has expressed concerns about meeting the tight deadline and the pricing of certain materials.

Business Writing Modality: In back and forth negotiations, address the vendor's objections sincerely and propose solutions that demonstrate flexibility and a willingness to collaborate. Show a proactive approach to resolving concerns and fostering a mutually beneficial partnership.

Example:

Dear [Recipient's Name],

Thank you for sharing your concerns regarding the pricing of materials and the tight deadline for the upcoming construction project. I understand the importance of adhering to budget constraints and delivering the project on time.

To address these concerns, we have reevaluated our budget and explored alternative sourcing options. We are committed to working within your specified budget while maintaining the highest quality standards. Additionally, our team is dedicated to streamlining the construction process and employing effective project management strategies to meet the deadline without compromising on excellence.

We believe that our collective expertise can pave the way for a successful partnership, and we remain open to further discussions to ensure that both our organizations benefit from this collaboration.

Looking forward to finding common ground and finalizing the details.

Best regards,
[Your Name]
Project Manager, [Your Company Name]

4. Confirming Agreements and Next Steps

Scenario: As a marketing manager, you have been negotiating with a potential advertising agency to execute a comprehensive marketing campaign for your company. After several rounds of discussions, you have reached an agreement on the scope and pricing.

Business Writing Modality: In back and forth negotiations, it is essential to formalize agreements and outline the next steps clearly. Ensure that both parties have a shared understanding of the terms and conditions to avoid misunderstandings in the future.

Example:
Dear [Recipient's Name],

I am pleased to inform you that we have successfully reached an agreement on the scope and pricing of the marketing campaign to be

executed by [Your Company Name]. Your team's creative approach and dedication to delivering impactful results were pivotal in solidifying this partnership.

To formalize our agreement, we kindly request you to review the attached contract, which outlines the campaign details, timelines, and terms. If everything aligns with our discussions, please sign and return a copy of the contract at your earliest convenience.

Once we receive the signed contract, our teams will immediately commence the planning and execution phases of the campaign. We anticipate a collaborative and successful journey ahead.

Thank you for your trust in [Your Company Name], and we are excited to embark on this venture together.

Best regards,
[Your Name]
Marketing Manager, [Your Company Name]

5. Expressing Gratitude and Maintaining Relationships

Scenario: After a series of negotiations, you have successfully secured a strategic partnership with a supplier for your retail business. The partnership promises a steady supply of high-quality products at competitive rates.

Business Writing Modality: In back and forth negotiations, expressing gratitude for the successful collaboration and maintaining positive relationships is crucial. Show appreciation for the supplier's flexibility and willingness to work together, setting the stage for potential future collaborations.

Example:
Dear [Recipient's Name],

On behalf of [Your Company Name], I want to extend my heartfelt gratitude for your cooperation and support throughout the negotiation process. Your flexibility and willingness to meet our requirements have been instrumental in solidifying this strategic partnership.

We are excited to begin working with your team to bring your high-quality products to our customers. Your reputation for excellence aligns perfectly with our commitment to delivering the best possible products and services to our loyal customer base.

As we commence this collaboration, I want to assure you that our team is fully committed to nurturing this partnership and ensuring its success. We believe that our collective efforts will lead to mutual growth and long-lasting prosperity.

Thank you once again, and we look forward to a productive and fruitful journey together.

Best regards,
[Your Name]
Purchasing Manager, [Your Company Name]

The Russell Brunson Email Sequence Formula

The Email Sequence Formula is a set of emails that can be used to create a steady stream of qualified leads for your business. It works by giving you a series of pre-written emails that you can use to start conversations with potential customers, and then, once they've been sufficiently impressed with your brand, offers them the opportunity to purchase from you.

The pre-sequence is the first email that you send to a prospect. It should be the most valuable email in your sequence, and it should be sent within 24 hours of their first interaction with you.

You want to ensure that this email stands out from everything else because it's going to be something special for them—so don't expect them to open any other emails from now on!

Sequence 1 for New Leads

This sequence is for new leads who have never bought from you before. The goal here is to get them to buy from you, so it's important that the email contains enough information about your products and services so they can decide if those are things they'd like to buy.

Make sure the subject line of this message makes it clear why someone should be interested in what you're offering.

Here's an example:

"Hey there! Thanks so much for filling out our form on [website]. We just want to make sure we're sending out emails that resonate with people—and yours did! If there's anything else we can do or clarify, please let us know at [email address]. Thanks again! Best wishes next time around."

The second email sequence is for existing customers. This is the most important part of your marketing strategy, because it's how you're going to get people hooked on your product or service. The goal here is to keep the relationship going and make them feel special while they're doing business with you. You can do this by using emails that offer special offers and discounts, but more importantly by giving them a reason to buy again—and keep coming back!

In this email, you'll get to ask for a testimonial and send out a freebie. This is an excellent time to ask for referrals because it's clear that your audience trusts you and wants more of what you have to offer.

The email sequence formula is a great way to get started on your own email marketing campaign. It's easy to implement, and will help you

develop an automated series of emails that can be used to communicate with your customers.

Who is Russel Brunson

Russell Brunson is a marketing wizard and has built an empire that generates millions of dollars in sales every month. He started his business back in 2012 when he launched Clickfunnels, but today he's better known for his other products like The Ultimate SaaS Product and Lazy Marketer podcasts. He's also known as an expert at creating sales funnels that get people excited about your brand so they can buy more stuff from you!

In the world of digital marketing, email remains a powerful tool for engaging with audiences, nurturing leads, and driving conversions. However, crafting effective email sequences that yield desirable results requires a strategic approach. Russell Brunson, a renowned marketer and co-founder of ClickFunnels, has devised an email sequence formula that has proven to be highly effective in driving engagement and conversions.\

Understanding the Russell Brunson Email Sequence Formula

The Russell Brunson Email Sequence Formula is designed to guide marketers through a series of emails that engage subscribers and lead

them through a carefully crafted sales funnel. It revolves around the principle of building a strong relationship with the audience, providing valuable content, and strategically introducing product offers at the right time.

1. The "Soap Opera" Sequence: Piquing Curiosity

The first part of the formula is the "Soap Opera" sequence, where the goal is to capture subscribers' attention and pique their curiosity. This sequence typically consists of two to three emails that tell a captivating story related to the product or service being offered. The story unfolds like an intriguing soap opera, leaving readers eager to know what happens next.

2. The "Epiphany Bridge" Sequence: Establishing Trust

Next comes the "Epiphany Bridge" sequence, where the focus is on establishing trust and authority. In this sequence, the marketer shares their personal journey, struggles, and insights that led them to discover the solution they are offering. By connecting on a personal level, the marketer builds credibility and positions themselves as an authority figure in their niche.

3. The "Daily Seinfeld" Sequence: Providing Value

The "Daily Seinfeld" sequence is all about providing consistent value to the audience. Named after the TV show "Seinfeld," known for its entertaining and engaging content, this sequence comprises daily emails that offer valuable tips, insights, and content related to the product or industry. The goal is to keep the audience engaged and interested in the marketer's expertise.

4. The "Closing" Sequence: Presenting the Offer

The "Closing" sequence is where the marketer introduces the product or service offer. By this stage, the audience has developed a strong connection with the marketer and perceives the value they bring. The offer is strategically presented, emphasizing the benefits and addressing any objections the audience may have.

5. The "Lost Lead" Sequence: Re-engaging Inactive Subscribers

The final part of the formula is the "Lost Lead" sequence, which focuses on re-engaging subscribers who did not convert during the previous sequences. This sequence aims to recapture their interest and encourage them to take action by offering additional incentives or bonuses.

The Russell Brunson Email Sequence Formula has garnered widespread popularity and acclaim for several reasons:

1. Storytelling Engages and Captivates

By incorporating storytelling elements in the "Soap Opera" and "Epiphany Bridge" sequences, the formula hooks the audience emotionally. Stories create a strong connection between the marketer and the subscriber, making them more receptive to the subsequent emails.

2. Consistent Value Builds Trust

The "Daily Seinfeld" sequence's daily emails keep the audience engaged and showcase the marketer's expertise. By consistently providing value, the marketer builds trust and positions themselves as a valuable resource.

3. Personalization Creates Relevance

The formula's emphasis on personalization ensures that each subscriber receives relevant content based on their interests and needs. This relevance fosters a sense of exclusivity and strengthens the relationship between the marketer and the audience.

4. Gradual Introduction of Offers

The gradual introduction of the product offer in the "Closing" sequence is crucial in preventing the audience from feeling

overwhelmed or "sold to." By this stage, the audience is more receptive to the offer due to the relationship built throughout the previous sequences.

5. Re-engagement Opportunities

The inclusion of the "Lost Lead" sequence allows marketers to re-engage inactive subscribers and potentially convert them into customers. This sequence provides a second chance to leverage the existing relationship and recapture the audience's interest.

The Russell Brunson Email Sequence Formula has proven to be highly effective in driving engagement, building relationships, and ultimately converting leads into customers. By strategically incorporating storytelling, consistent value, personalization, and gradual offer introduction, the formula capitalizes on the power of email marketing to its fullest potential. Marketers who adopt this formula can create compelling email sequences that resonate with their audience and lead to tangible business results.

Ready to see what the email series would look like?

1. Sample Email for the "Soap Opera" Sequence: Piquing Curiosity

Subject: The Untold Story Behind Our Revolutionary Product Launch 🎬

Dear [Subscriber's Name],

I hope this email finds you well. Today, I want to share a story that has been kept a secret until now. It's the thrilling tale of how our team embarked on a journey to revolutionize the [Your Industry] landscape.

As I write this, memories from the early days of our project come rushing back. The countless sleepless nights, the exhilarating breakthroughs, and the unforeseen challenges that tested our determination to the core.

But enough about me - what about you? Have you ever wondered how [Your Industry] can be transformed for the better? If you have, I encourage you to join us on this incredible adventure.

Tomorrow, I'll reveal the next chapter of our story and introduce you to the groundbreaking solution that will redefine [Your Industry].

Stay tuned and be ready to witness the birth of something extraordinary.

Best regards,

[Your Name]

[Your Title]

[Your Company Name]

[Your Contact Information]

2. Sample Email for the "Epiphany Bridge" Sequence: Establishing Trust

Subject: From Struggles to Success: My Journey to Solving [Industry] Challenges ✴

Dear [Subscriber's Name],

I hope this email finds you inspired and ready to seize new opportunities. Today, I want to share a personal story that shaped my passion for solving [Industry] challenges and led me to the groundbreaking solution I'm offering.

Years ago, I faced countless obstacles in [Your Industry], just like you may be experiencing today. I was frustrated by the lack of efficient solutions and felt discouraged by the barriers holding me back.

However, in the midst of these struggles, I had an epiphany. I realized that true innovation comes from daring to think differently. This revelation fueled my determination to create a transformative solution that addresses [Industry] pain points head-on.

Today, I stand before you with a solution that has the potential to revolutionize your [Industry] experience. I invite you to join me on this journey, where we can empower each other to achieve greatness.

Tomorrow, I'll reveal how our solution can transform your [Industry] challenges into opportunities for growth and success.

Looking forward to sharing more with you soon!

Best regards,
[Your Name]
Founder, [Your Company Name]
[Your Contact Information]

3. Sample Email for the "Daily Seinfeld" Sequence: Providing Value

Subject: Discover the [Your Industry] Tips You've Been Missing Out On 📑

Dear [Subscriber's Name],

Happy [Day of the Week]! I hope this email adds a dose of positivity and value to your day.

Today, I want to share a little-known [Your Industry] tip that can significantly boost your productivity and enhance your results. 🚀

Have you ever found yourself struggling to [Common Industry Challenge]? I've been there too, and I'm excited to show you a simple yet effective technique that has transformed how I tackle this challenge.

[Tip of the Day: Provide a concise and actionable tip that aligns with your expertise.]

Remember, success in [Your Industry] comes from consistently applying small, actionable strategies that compound over time.

Stay tuned for more valuable insights and actionable tips to empower your [Your Industry] journey!

Best regards,
[Your Name]
[Your Title]
[Your Company Name]
[Your Contact Information]

4. Sample Email for the "Closing" Sequence: Presenting the Offer

Subject: Unlock Your Full Potential with Our Exclusive [Product/Service] Offer 💎

Dear [Subscriber's Name],

I hope this email finds you excited about the possibilities ahead. After weeks of unveiling our journey and sharing valuable insights, we're finally ready to present the key that unlocks your full potential.

Introducing our exclusive [Product/Service], meticulously designed to address the exact challenges you face in [Your Industry]. With this solution, you can:

[Benefit 1]

[Benefit 2]

[Benefit 3]

We've carefully crafted this offer to cater to your unique needs, and we're confident that it will deliver the results you desire.

To ensure you don't miss out on this limited-time opportunity, we've included a special discount for our valued subscribers. But remember, this offer won't last forever.

Click the link below to discover how [Product/Service] can transform your [Your Industry] journey:

[CTA Button: "Unlock Your Potential"]

Take a leap towards success with [Your Company Name]!

Best regards,

[Your Name]

[Your Title]

[Your Company Name]

[Your Contact Information]

5. Sample Email for the "Lost Lead" Sequence: Re-engaging Inactive Subscribers

Subject: Your [Product/Service] Journey Continues - Don't Miss Out! 🚀

Dear [Subscriber's Name],

We hope this email finds you well. It's been a while since our last communication, and we miss you!

As one of our valued subscribers, you've been on an incredible [Your Industry] journey with us. We've shared captivating stories, valuable insights, and exciting offers to help you achieve your goals.

We understand that life gets busy, and you may have had other priorities. But we want you to know that your success in [Your Industry] is still our top priority.

To get back on track and continue your [Your Industry] transformation, we've prepared a special surprise just for you.

[Re-engagement Offer: Offer an exclusive incentive or bonus to re-ignite interest.]

Let's pick up where we left off and continue this incredible journey together. Click the link below to claim your exclusive offer:

[CTA Button: "Claim Your Offer"]

We can't wait to help you reach new heights in [Your Industry].

Best regards,
[Your Name]
[Your Title]
[Your Company Name]
[Your Contact Information]

Note: Ensure to customize the samples based on your industry, expertise, and specific offers to maximize effectiveness.

The Continuum

Congratulations!

You have reached the final chapter of "The Business Email Writing Guide." Throughout this journey, we have explored the art and science of crafting powerful and persuasive business emails. You've learned the essential elements of a successful email, mastered the art of effective subject lines, and understood the nuances of tone and etiquette.

In this conclusive chapter, we will tie all the knowledge together and equip you with the tools to become a confident and proficient business email writer. Whether you are a seasoned professional or just starting your career, the principles discussed in this guide will undoubtedly elevate your communication skills and make a lasting impact on your recipients.

1. The Power of Clarity and Conciseness

In business email writing, clarity is paramount. Avoid ambiguity and be precise in your messaging. Clearly state the purpose of your email in the first few sentences, so your recipients know what to expect.

Keep your sentences and paragraphs concise to maintain the reader's attention and prevent information overload.

2. The Importance of Personalization

Personalized emails are more engaging and build stronger connections with recipients. Address your recipients by their names and take the time to understand their specific needs and interests. Tailor your emails to resonate with their individual preferences, which will demonstrate that you value and respect their time.

3. Embracing Professional Tone and Etiquette

Professionalism in your emails leaves a lasting impression on your recipients. Use a respectful and polite tone, avoiding any language that could be perceived as offensive or unprofessional. Always proofread your emails for grammar and spelling errors, and ensure that your email signature includes relevant contact information.

4. Building Trust through Transparency

Transparency is the foundation of trust in business relationships. Be honest and straightforward in your emails, especially when it comes to discussing challenges or setbacks. This level of transparency will foster trust and credibility, positioning you as a reliable and trustworthy professional.

5. Timing and Follow-up

Pay attention to the timing of your emails. Consider your recipients' time zones and work schedules to optimize the chances of them reading your emails promptly. Follow up on important emails after a reasonable period, but avoid excessive follow-ups that may come across as intrusive.

6. The Art of Effective Subject Lines

Subject lines can make or break the open rates of your emails. Craft subject lines that are attention-grabbing, relevant, and accurately reflect the email's content. Experiment with different subject line techniques and analyze their performance to improve your email open rates over time.

7. Engaging Storytelling for Impact

Incorporating storytelling elements in your emails can make your messages more memorable and relatable. Share relevant anecdotes or case studies to illustrate your points and connect with your audience on an emotional level. Storytelling humanizes your emails, making them more compelling and impactful.

8. Tailoring Emails for Specific Goals

Customize your emails based on the specific goals you aim to achieve. Whether it's persuading a client to sign a contract, seeking feedback from a colleague, or thanking a business partner for their support, tailor your emails accordingly to maximize their effectiveness.

9. Measuring and Iterating for Improvement

Analyze the performance of your emails using data and metrics. Measure open rates, click-through rates, and response rates to understand what resonates with your audience. Continuously iterate and improve your email writing skills based on these insights.

10. The Ongoing Journey of Growth

Remember, mastering business email writing is an ongoing journey of growth and refinement. Embrace every opportunity to communicate professionally and persuasively. Seek feedback from colleagues, mentors, or clients to gain valuable insights and continuously enhance your skills.

As you conclude "The Business Email Writing Guide," you are now equipped with the knowledge and strategies to craft compelling, persuasive, and effective business emails. With every email you write, remember the power of clarity, personalization, and professionalism.

Your emails have the potential to drive business outcomes, build relationships, and create a lasting impact.

As you embark on your professional journey, let your business emails be a reflection of your expertise, integrity, and dedication to excellence. Be fearless in expressing your ideas and insights, and always remember the immense value of effective communication in today's fast-paced business landscape.

Best regards,
Abi Demi.

References

Guffey, M. E., & Loewy, D. (2017). Essentials of Business Communication (11th ed.). Cengage Learning.

Hemmingway, E. (2018). The Hemmingway Editor. Retrieved from https://hemingwayapp.com/

Hirst, G., & Harrison, J. (2014). The Communication Handbook (5th ed.). Routledge.

Purdue Online Writing Lab. (n.d.). Email Etiquette for Students. Retrieved from https://owl.purdue.edu/owl/general_writing/email_etiquette_for_stud ents/index.html

Schwalbe, K. (2018). Information Technology Project Management (9th ed.). Cengage Learning.

Singh, M., & Singh, M. . Essential English for Business Communication. PHI Learning Private Limited.

Richard Johnson-Sheehan. (2017). Technical Communication Today (6th ed.).

Turabian, K. L. (2007). A Manual for Writers of Research Papers, Theses, and Dissertations (7th ed.). University of Chicago Press.

Writing Center, University of North Carolina at Chapel Hill. (n.d.). Email Etiquette. Retrieved from https://writingcenter.unc.edu/tips-and-tools/email-etiquette/